THE DICHOTOMY:
FACTS AND PERCEPTIONS

A Recipe For Social Cohesion

LENKWANE HENRY MATHUNYANE

Be conscientious – Build a nation. Make a
contribution- Accomplish immortality.

Copyright © 2022 by Lenkwane Henry Mathunyane

Hardback: 978-1-959082-21-7
Paperback: 978-1-959082-00-2
eBook: 978-1-959082-01-9
Library of Congress Control Number: 2022914061

All rights reserved. No part of this publication may be reproduced, distributed, or transmitted in any form or by any electronic or mechanical means, without the prior written permission of the publisher, except in the case of brief quotations embodied in critical reviews and certain other noncommercial uses permitted by copyright law.

This is a work of nonfiction.

Ordering Information:

BookTrail Agency
8838 Sleepy Hollow Rd.
Kansas City, MO 64114

Printed in the United States of America

TABLE OF CONTENTS

Foreword 1
Preface 3
Acknowledgements 5

Chapter 1 Life and the Universe 7

1.1 Human existence and Survival......................................8
1.2 A spiritual person... 13
1.3 The foundation of the Christian belief. 14
1.4 The Objectives of Christian Education. 14
1.5 Education, becoming, and learning 15
1.6 Educational implications in relation to teaching
and learning in the religious life world............................ 17
    1.6.1 The need for religion in the educational
    milieu of the adolescent child 17
    1.6.2 The value of religion to the adolescent child...... 18
    1.6.3 Changes in religious interest and effects on
    behaviour 18
1.7 Synthesis.. 19

Chapter 2 Man and the life world 20

2.1 Man, the Moral being... 21
2.2 Religion and morality.. 21
2.3 Special attributes, ethics, and values 22
    2.3.1 Special attributes...22
    2.3.2 Ethics 22
    2.3.3 Values...23
    2.3.3 Moral values in human development 24
2.4 Educational implications for teaching and learning
in the moral development of the adolescent child 25
    2.4.1 Moral development 25
    2.4.2 Factors influencing the adolescent's morals........26

  2.4.2.1 Parental influence 26
  2.4.2.1 Sexual roles 27
  2.4.2.3 Peer group conformity 27
  2.4.2. 4 Moral values from a traditional African perspective 27
  2.4.2. 5 The educational process in the life world of a traditional African child 28
 2.5 Synthesis 31

Chapter 3 Leadership within democracy 32

 3.1 The establishment of governance structures 33
 3.2 Democracy..34
 3.3 Role players in democracy..35
  3.3.1 Church organisations, civil society, and the state..35
  3.3.2 The responsibilities of civilians and Christians towards the state 36
 3.4 Leadership 37
 3.4.1 The empowered leader 37
  3.4.2 Effective leaders 38
   3.4.2.1 The innate characteristics of leaders...........39
   3.4.2.2 Qualities portraying the true image of a servant-leader..40
   3.4.2.3 The recreational leader................................. 41
 3.5 Educational implications for teaching and learning within a Democracy 42
  3.5.1 The establishment of a positive educational climate in a democratic school environment...............43
  3.5.2 Educational induction into society 44
  3.5.3 The role of leadership in school excellence 46
 3.6 Synthesis **46**

Chapter 4 The life theatre 47

 4.1 Arts and worship..48
 4.2 Religious and traditional rituals and healing............51

4.2.1 The healing ministry 51
4.2.2 Spiritual or faith healing 52
4.2.3 Christian healing 54
4.2.4 The use of drugs in religious and traditional healing 55
4.2.5 The relationship between traditional medicine and Western biotechnology 55
4.3 Sports: The international language 60
4.4 The driver of life: Life skills 61
4.5 The educational implications for learning and teaching within the theatrical life world 63
4.6 Synthesis 66

Chapter 5 Social development 68

5.1 The process of socialisation 69
5.2 Erik Erikson's psychosocial development theory 72
5.3 The family **76**
   5.3.1 The role of the family 76
      5.3.1.1 General functions 76
      5.3.1.2 Supplementary functions 77
      5.3.1.3 General features 77
      5.3.1.4 Parental practices affecting child development 78
   5.3.2 Procreation: Sexuality in the family 78
   5.3.3 The father, the head of the family 79
   5.3.4 Parents' (father and mother) relationship 80
   5.3.5 The role of the extended family 81
5.4 Family relationships 82
   5.4.1 Children and the home 82
      5.4.1.1 Older siblings in the family 84
      5.4.1.2 Grandparents 85
      5.4.1.3 The influence of tradition and culture in the family 86
5.5 Friendships 86
   5.5.1 Sociality 87

    5.5.2 Play, the best teacher 88
    5.5.3 The influence of a peer group in child development 89
    5.5.4 The development of heterosexual relationships 91
    5.5.5 The influence of tradition and culture in the peer group 92
5.6 Educational implications for teaching and learning in a culturally diverse life world 93
    5.6.1 The principles of teaching and learning in a culturally diverse school environment 95
        5.6.1.1 The principle of differentiation 96
        5.6.1.2 The principle of integration 96
        5.6.1.3 The principle of continuity 96
        5.6.1.4 The principle of assimilation 97
    5.6.2 Objectives of education in a cultural diverse society 97
        5.6.2.1 General objectives of education in a culturally diverse society 98
        5.6.2.2 Specific objectives of education in a multicultural society 100
    5.6.3 Creation of a psychologically safe learning environment 102
        5.6.3.1 Teachers: Excellence in action 102
        5.6.3.2 Community education 104
    5.6.4 The collaboration of the 'trio' (home, general community, and s chool) towards successful learning 105
5.7 Synthesis 108

REFERENCES 110

FOREWORD

This work on various human developmental aspects begins at the beginning of all things. The author has demonstrated a sound understanding of the essence of the truth about creation and its purpose.

He points out that coexistence is an in born human element. Put differently, a human being is a gregarious being. View it from whatever angle, the fact remains that God regarded his own work unfinished if he did not embellish it by introducing companionship/relationships.

The author goes at length by demonstrating requirements for a harmonious, smooth and sustained relationships within a diverse, religious and cultural dynamics in the life - world of humankind.

This work is a life - long orientation and a foundation for nation building. It focuses right in the classroom by providing each child with the relevant life skills and equips educators with various teaching strategies. 'No wonder' it is strongly recommended as a 'must have' school hand book.

Parents and the community at large are motivated and their much needed support is solicited for a successful teaching and learning, the outputs of which is a prosperous nation.

The Editor.

PREFACE

Overview of the contents

The contents of this handy book reflect on subjects that would enable parents, teachers, and students to broaden and deepen their insight in the interdependences of human beings in the social environment.

Subjects like psychosocial development, education, religion, leadership, and tradition feature prominently as indispensible interrelated life aspects that complement one another for human coexistence.

The concept of dichotomy only seeks to highlight that in a diverse society, apart from the prevailing similarities, there are also differences, which enrich the nation and have to be appreciated and celebrated. The subject matter is structured in such a way that it is reader-friendly. Keywords and key phrases used have been highlighted, explained, and described in order to facilitate a mellow understanding of the subject matter. The educational implications in all subjects have been presented as guidance and a well-crafted life orientation towards successful teaching and learning. Syntheses have been provided in order to refresh the mind of the reader on what he had read. The author at the beginning of each chapter and some paragraphs has drawn from the voices of great men and women who, through their powerful influence, changed the world.

This informative and educative book is compiled as a resource for students, and teachers in service at the teaching and learning centres— namely, high schools, tertiary institutions, public and private colleges.

ACKNOWLEDGEMENTS

I would like to acknowledge the support, guidance, and assistance of the following individuals; Lenkwane Modiba for his typing skills; my wife Thandiwe Regina for her unending patience. A special appreciation to my grandchildren; Terry, Meladi, Tshireletso, Sibongakonke, Boipelo, Tshegofatso and Boikgantsho; who surrounded me with pencils and papers, also saying are writing like their grandfather. I hope this work will inspire them to make a positive contribution in the life of others.

Name: Lenkwane Henry Mathunyane
Place: Mhluzi
Date: 2020

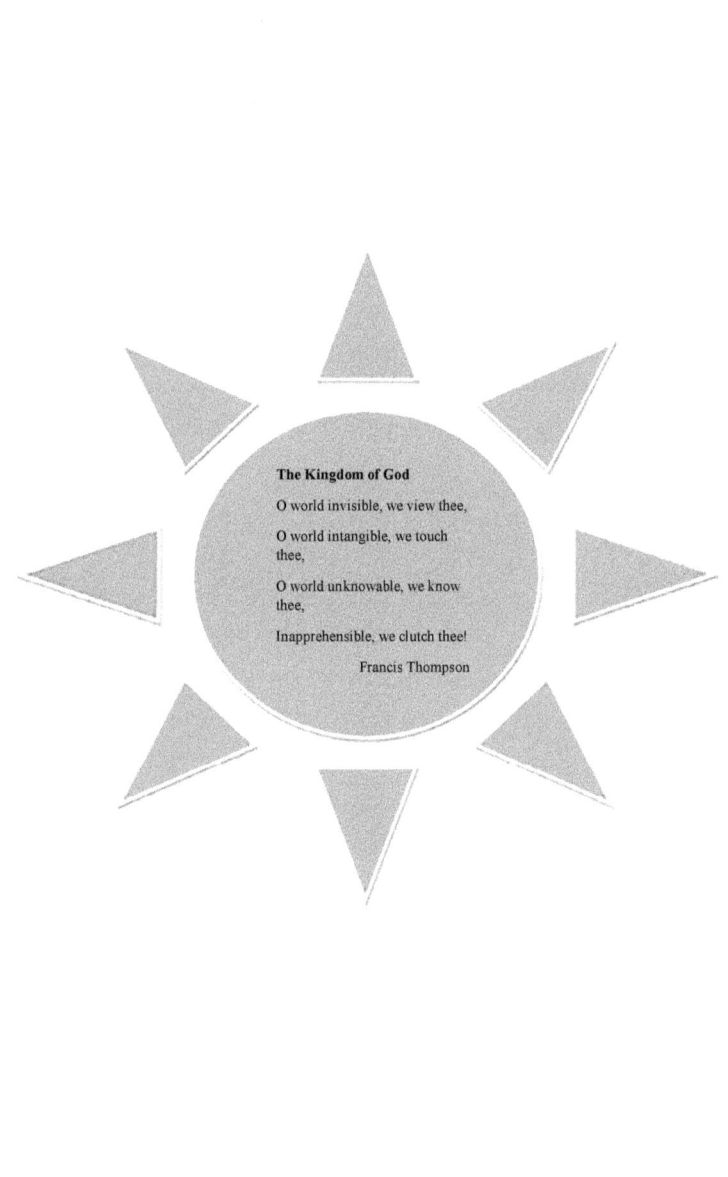

The Kingdom of God

O world invisible, we view thee,

O world intangible, we touch thee,

O world unknowable, we know thee,

Inapprehensible, we clutch thee!

                Francis Thompson

CHAPTER 1

LIFE AND THE UNIVERSE

The Origin of the World and Life was no accident. There is a Creator: God.

John Taylor

Subjects

1.1 Human existence and survival
1.2 A Spiritual person
1.3 The foundation of the Christian belief
1.4 The Objectives of Christian education
1.5 Education, becoming and learning
1.6 Educational implications in relation to teaching and learning in the religious life world
1.6.1. The need for religion in the educational milieu of the adolescent child
1.6.2. The value of religion to the adolescent child
1.6.3. Changes in religious interest and effects on behaviour
1.7 Synthesis

> **Keywords**
>
> *Moral being, Allah, Religion, spiritual person, spiritual being, sacredness of life, Christian Education*

1.1 Human existence and Survival

Human existence and survival including the conditions of life, namely, space, time, emotions, and many experiences – give birth to society, culture, faith or religion.

A society is a comprehensive social grouping and includes all institutions needed for human survival. The way of life of a society is referred to as culture. Society and culture are interdependent, and culture exists only as an aspect of society (Stark 1975: 37).

The terms *plural* and *multi* mean "more than one or many", and therefore, the terms *cultural pluralism* and *multiculturalism* are frequently used interchangeably (compare Fowler and Fowler 1969).

Cultural pluralism involves the mutual exchange of cultural contents, respect for different views, and the belief that the cultures of different groups enrich a nation and provides it with alternative ways to view the world (Mathunyane 1996:11).

Multiculturalism implies that all people are members of their societies and that they are conditioned by their surroundings and culture. Multiculturalism discourages people from having any inherent bias against other cultures but encourages people to find interest in the different world views (Oliver 1990:26).

Socialization is defined as the process by which individuals learn to conform to the moral standard, role expectations, and requirements of acceptable behavior of the community. Put differently, socialization is the process whereby children become members of the community in that they learn:

THE DICHOTOMY: FACTS AND PERCEPTIONS

- √ to behave according to the values and norms of the community
- √ to learn how to get on with others and what changes are to be made in order to fit into society (Craig 1983: 12; Prinsloo and Du Plesis 1998:11).

All religious systems are based on the world view in relation to the existence of man. Religion is important to human beings in the following ways:

- It involves the whole person, mind, heart, and imagination.
- It is a moral, philosophical, and social aspect of people. Therefore, a personal religion denotes an individual's emotional response to the power that rules the universe, a faith and hope to which a person can cling to in uncertain circumstances—namely, when under threat, sad, sick, and troubled.
- It is also based on the belief and practices or religious observances, which are meaningful and helpful, and observed in common with others of the same faith (compare Vrey 1979: 182; Lerner and Spanier 1980: 66; Keeley 1982: 358).

In broad terms, if you mention religion, you touch the depth of the whole person. The points alluded to suggest that religion is a very delicate affair to be approached with much sensitivity.

There are a number of faiths or religions. Amongst many are Judaism, Hinduism, Islam, Christianity, and so on.

In these religious practices, prayer is a means of communication with the Supreme Being. There is no uniform way of praying but what remains is that the words uttered or actions made, bring the required intervention of the power of the universe.

- Judaism is a belief in God, the Creator—the living, the faithful, and the righteous God. Jews strongly believe that God speaks and listens at the same time. They declare, 'The Lord our God is one Lord.' The law of God, Torah, is captured in the first five books of the Bible, which regulates the conduct of every Jew.

Torah scroll

Hinduism maintains that all people are able to move closer to God. In the process of getting nearer to God, man is led to the ultimate goal—that of the soul reuniting with the supreme reality. On the whole, Hinduism is characterised by the following outlook:

- They worship some visible form of the divine for help.
- Theirs is the religion of incarnation; the worshipper has a mental picture of the one he worships.
- They believe in a personal god. Their god, who is personal, is spoken to and listens when they pray. Hinduism also asserts that the true god is unlimited in the sense that he never changes and is available at all times.

THE DICHOTOMY: FACTS AND PERCEPTIONS

A woman offering prayers

- Islam is a way of life. Islam is the driver/pilot of every aspect of life in the social, economic, political, ethical, and aesthetic world. The Islamic creed proclaims that 'there is no other god but Allah'. Mohammed is the prophet of Allah. Allah has power over all things and is a compassionate and merciful god. Faith in Allah, the creator, means a total submission to his will.

"Ramadan oil lamps"

- In Christianity, Christians believe in God, the Creator, and that God revealed himself through Christ, who alone is the way, the truth, and the life.

God created heaven and earth. Man became the climax of his creation and inherited his image (Genesis 1:1, 27). The inheritance of the image or the likeness of God established a special relationship with him and makes man a reasoning, moral, and creative creature.

Creation was completed in six days. John Taylor (Alexander and Alexander 1973: 127) gives a summary of the perceived sequence of events as follows:

Day 1: Light and darkness (day and night) were created.
Day 2: Earth's atmosphere was created.
Day 3: Dry land (plants and trees) and seas were created;
Day 4: The sun, moon, stars, seasons, days, and years were created.

Day 5: Sea creatures and birds were created.
Day 6: Land animals and mankind were created; creation was completed.
Day 7: God took a respite and reflected on the whole creation. In his reflection and evaluation, God was satisfied by the orderliness and simplicity of how he created everything, and he declared that he will continue with the maintenance and sustenance of his creation.

God is a spiritual being, super- and extrahuman. This is the god, the creator, and the sustainer of the universe, whom all mankind believe in. The belief of mankind and his views are based on a supreme value, God. The entire human way of life is determined by faith. Faith is based on trust in God. Our reliance in God is the belief and hope that God is trustworthy and will fulfil his promises.

1.2 A spiritual person.

Christianity is based on these beliefs:

- ➢ Man is a moral being.
- ➢ The voice of conscience is a reflection of internalised and external moral laws.
- ➢ God reveals the divine truth through his Son, Jesus Christ.
- ➢ Man is destined for life beyond the grave; his life is a preparation.
- ➢ God is omnipresent; he is present everywhere at the same time.
- ➢ God is omnipotent; he has unlimited power, great power.
- ➢ God is omniscient; he knows everything (Redden and Ryan 1956: 181).

The power of God to see and know (in advance) all that happens or will happen, good or bad, demonstrates that God is the alpha and the omega. David testified to this fact by saying, 'You saw me before I was born; the days allocated to me had all been recorded in your book, before any of them ever began' (Psalm 139: 16).

Apostle Paul corroborates and points out that man has been elected and predestined to eternal life long before the foundation of the world was laid. Man has been chosen to be his through his union with Christ (Ephesians 1:4–5).

1.3 The foundation of the Christian belief.

'Spirituality is a way of being and experiences that comes about through awareness of a transcendent dimension characterised by certain identifiable values in regard to self, others, nature and life' (Elkins et al. 1988: 10).

A spiritual person is identifiable by the following characteristics:

- He endeavours to make life meaningful because he understands and knows that he exists for a purpose.
- He is visionary and committed to social justice.
- He believes that life is infused with sacredness.
- He believes in *botho*. He is his brother's keeper.
- He can appreciate material things, such as money and possessions, but does not seek satisfaction from them.

1.4 The Objectives of Christian Education.

The objectives of Christian education, amongst others, are to produce true Christians. A true Christian is a person whose aspects of life are driven and based on the belief that God revealed himself to us through Jesus Christ, who alone is the way, the truth, and the life.

Christianity is a way of life to be lived and is a work of authority, a work of love, following Jesus Christ as an example.

Christian churches carry the command of preaching the gospel to all mankind and are therefore dominated by sermons, penitence, the fear of God, faith in Christ, the righteousness of faith, comfort, prayer, the cross, and so forth.

Finally, Christianity aims at producing a community, society, and church whose thoughts are dominated by:

- bearing one another's burdens
- correcting one another
- comforting
- edifying one another
- togetherness
- humility
- a softened heart for the poor and afflicted
- worshipping with other believers.

These, with God on our side, will lead to the ultimate or desired goals of Christianity.

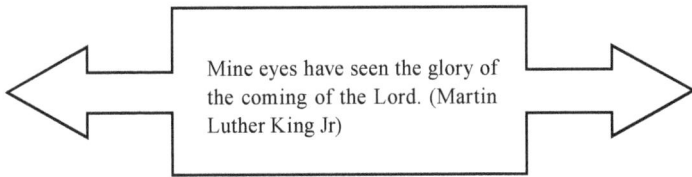

Mine eyes have seen the glory of the coming of the Lord. (Martin Luther King Jr)

1.5 Education, becoming, and learning

Pius (1936: 26) writes: 'The younger generation must be trained in the arts and science for the advantage and prosperity of civil society. Therefore, it is necessary for society to create a social institution, the school.' The primary concern of the school is the installation of all basic experiences, attitudes, and concepts which are essential to adult life and therefore provides education (Stone 1981: 19).

Education is a process in which the society's knowledge, norms, customs, social values, and skills are transmitted from one generation to another. Traditional systems are educational and play a role in the transmission of customs from generation to generation (compare Kavanagh 2002: 1244; Le Roux and Pretorius 1992: 8).

Becoming and learning are interactive and interdependent. Becoming is an innate desire to improve oneself—that is, a need to achieve according to one's abilities and to self-actualise.

Learning is a process in which the child's 'intellectual faculties take precedence over other psychological activities' (Vrey 1979: 20).

In other words, in learning, a person acquires knowledge and skills. Knowledge acquisition is accompanied by a behavioural change (the change in behaviour, namely, a change of what is known for the better), and the person commands power—*tsebo ke matla* or 'knowledge is power'. This power in most circumstances and new situations is applied successfully. The empowered person is expected to be of value and worth to society (compare Mathunyane 1992: 12–13; Garrison and Archer 2000: 39; and Kegan 2000: 49).

Education is on the whole a process of guiding a child towards self-actualisation, and continuous interactions between the child, adult, and the environment prevail. As alluded to earlier, education, becoming, and learning are interactive and interdependent activities (Le roux 1993: 100–101).

1.6 Educational implications in relation to teaching and learning in the religious life world

A life world of a person is the whole landscape—all relationships with the self, objects, ideas, and people; the cultural domain; and the integration of what is seen, heard, felt, and used.

Life is dynamic; hence, the life world expands as new interests and ideas develop. Therefore, a person makes the life world habitable for himself. (compare Smit and Kilian in Oberholzer et al. 1993: 156; Van den Aardweg and Yan den Aardweg 1988: 141).

1.6.1 The need for religion in the educational milieu of the adolescent child

A child needs religion, a belief that he can accept, and observances that are meaningful and helpful to him.

A child needs a religion that gives him faith in life, a faith to live by, and a faith that can help him learn to withstand the conflicts and doubts he sometimes have.

1.6.2 The value of religion to the adolescent child

Religion touches the heart and directs and moulds life in one or more of the following ways:

- √ Religion is a moral, philosophical, and social institution.
- √ A child who rates religion as being important shows a high level of religious commitment as well as commitment towards religious institutions.
- √ Students meet the academic and social expectations of the school more than non-religious students do (Mathunyane 1992: 48; Lerner and Spanier 1980: 66; and Santrock 1984: 536).

1.6.3 Changes in religious interest and effects on behaviour

As children grow older, they begin to question religious concepts and beliefs in their childhood. Religious doubt or religious questioning will emerge.

Religious doubt involves the following:

- There is confusion and uncertainty and a decrease in religious observances.
- This gradually develops into a religious awakening that leads to a reconstruction of religious beliefs and attitudes. Many boys and girls decide to dedicate their lives to serve their church and become extremely enthusiastic about religious activities.

Reawakening influences changes in religious beliefs and attitudes. The child may adopt one or any combination of the following:

- There is less interest in religion and religious observances.
- In the main, the adolescent is likely to retain the faith of his childhood (family faith).
- In the extreme, the adolescent is likely to adopt another faith that is different in most respects from that of his parents (Mathunyane 1992: 50).

1.7 Synthesis

God is a spiritual being; he is the creator and sustainer of the universe. The entire human way of life is determined by faith and the belief of the omnipresence, omnipotence, and omniscience of God.

A spiritual person is a person who believes in a transcendent dimension of life, knows the purpose of life, believes in the sacredness of life, and lives a life full of love.

The next chapter will deal with man, the moral being, and his life world.

CHAPTER 2

MAN AND THE LIFE WORLD

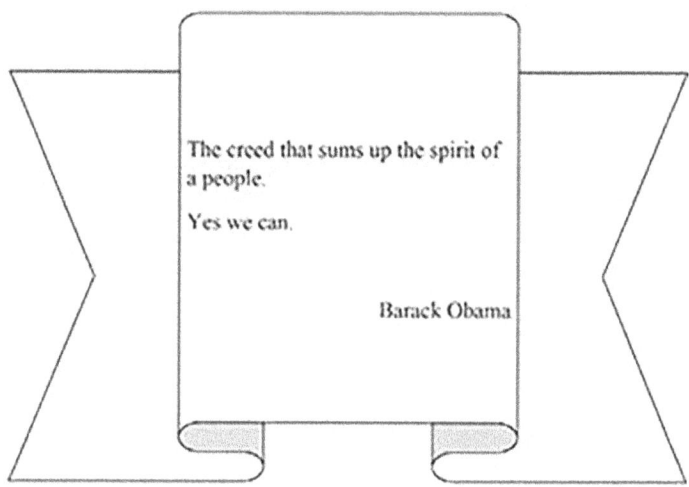

The creed that sums up the spirit of a people.

Yes we can.

Barack Obama

Subjects

2.1 Man, the moral being
2.2 Religion and morality
2.3 Special attributes, ethics, and values
2.4 Educational implications for teaching and learning in the moral development of the adolescent child
2.5 Synthesis

> **Key concepts**
>
> Mortal being, morality, special attributes, ethics, values, immortal being, love, hedonism, moral development, cognitive approach, affective approach, social approach, traditional African values, traditional African children.

2.1 Man, the Moral being

The pure creation produced an immortal being, a human being. It is God's will that even today, the world is blessed with newly born souls. This is an indication that we live by the will of God, and therefore, no one is allowed to kill or to take his life.

It became unfortunate when man violated God's instructions and ended up with the introduction of death. This was the birth of a mortal being (Psalm 78:39). Jesus Christ alone is immortal.

In order to save the world, God displayed his love by sending his only Son, Jesus Christ, who has revealed immortal life by ending the power of death (2 Timothy 1:10). Man has no share or role in the action of being saved but through faith alone. This faith is the foundation of the belief that man is a moral, the voice of conscience, a reflection of internalised and external moral law.

2.2 Religion and morality

Religion consists of two elements—namely, a faith which is based on the individual's beliefs and, secondly, practices or religious observances in common with others of the same faith.

Morals are standards of right or wrong. This exposition suggests that moral education and religion are inseparable.

2.3 Special attributes, ethics, and values

2.3.1 Special attributes

Only human beings can differentiate between right (good) and wrong (evil) on the basis of an ethical position are free and therefore need to act responsibly, and are capable of faith, the only beings that exist in relation to God, self, other people, and the world. In all these relationships, God gave human beings a law, that of *love*.

2.3.2 Ethics

In the attributes mentioned, it is said human beings differentiated between wrong and right based on an ethical position. Ethics are based on certain basic principles, namely:

- ➢ The only thing that is intrinsically good is *love*.
- ➢ Christians' decisions are guided by love.
- ➢ Love and justice are inseparable.
- ➢ Love is extended to one's neighbour.
- ➢ Love influences decisions in various situations.

This love has been demonstrated by God in that he so loved the whole world that he gave his only Son so that everyone who believes in him may not perish but may have eternal life (John 3:16). God continued to say that he is love and those who abide in love abide in him as he abides in them (1 John 4:16), and he concluded by saying, 'Love your neighbour as you love yourself' (Roman 13:9). Loving one's neighbour equates to botho.

Botho is a social contract that originates in the individual family and spreads to the entire community as an extended family network. *Motho ke motho ka batho* means that 'a person is a person through other people within his specific community'. 'I am because you are, you are because we are' (compare Keeley 1982: 287; Van Deventer and Kruger 2003: 71).

2.3.3 Values

Rokeach, Kluckhom and Von Bertalanffy (Bergh et al. 1999: 192–194) define *value* as 'an enduring belief that a certain mode of conduct is personally or socially preferable, and also defined as an implicit or explicit conception of the desirable, which influences behavioural choices'. Also, values are functional in one of the most activities of humans, that of creating a symbolic world.

For illustration purposes, an example of a set of values is presented as:

- self-discipline: persevering in achieving goals and being able to control behaviour,
- healthy lifestyle: taking care of yourself and avoiding anything harmful and refusing the use of drugs
- respect: taking care of the needs, beliefs, and feelings of others
- kindness: exhibiting care and concern for your fellow man
- responsibility: taking responsibility for your actions
- honesty: being truthful and trustworthy
- commitment : being good in the service you render to people
- courage: standing firm to your values in the face of challenges (Engelbrecht et al. 1996: 297).

In everyday life, situations vary, and a consistent application of these values is imperative. Therefore, the changing world demands versatility (without compromise) in facing challenges that emerge as a result of developments in the social, political, economic, and cultural fronts.

2.3.3 Moral values in human development

Interactions which demand the application of moral values include, amongst others, fun and situational, authentic, and convenient (free to all) encounters (Gerdes et al. 1981: 149–150).

- ➢ Fun encounter is a situation where one is not seriously committed to the relationship, and a person tends to become too casual and careless with no intended results,
- ➢ Situational encounter is the judgement of a situation according to
- ➢ your own standards.
- ➢ Authentic encounter is an encounter that aims at producing people's dignity, identity, and self-confident personalities.
- ➢ Hedonism is acting without following any standard in terms of choosing what is pleasurable now irrespective of the long-term results.

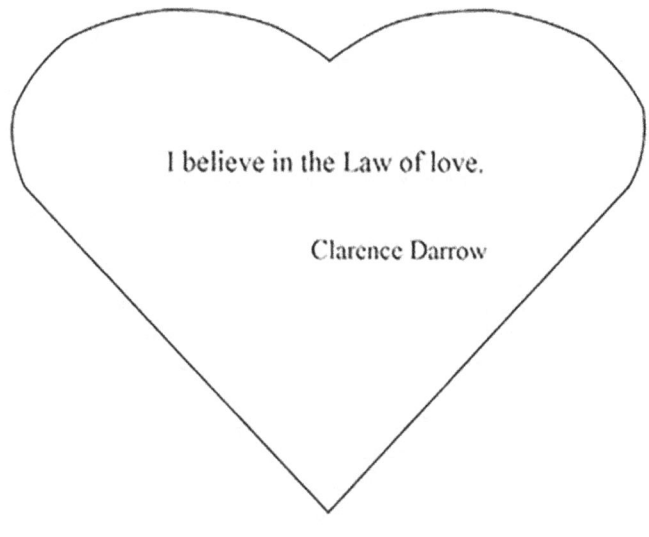

I believe in the Law of love.

Clarence Darrow

2.4 Educational implications for teaching and learning in the moral development of the adolescent child

2.4.1 Moral development

Moral development concerns rules and conventions about acceptable behaviour often in relation to a person's interactions with other people.

There are three basic approaches—namely, cognitive, affective, and social approaches—employed towards understanding moral development.

The cognitive view of moral development focuses on moral reasoning and considers cognitive development to be a necessary stimulant for changes in the stages of moral development.

The affective perspective on moral development focuses on the role of empathy, sympathy, and guilt, which are thought to be influenced by socialisation (Santrock 1984: 524).

The social perspective views morality as linked primarily to friendship experiences and the related sense of togetherness (Rogers 1985: 161).

A fully developed individual's morality is identifiable by singling out the following observations:

- The person is able to recognise the sensitivity of issues in a given social situation.
- The person is able to determine what ought to be done in a given situation.
- The person stands firm to his values, and his actions are always influenced by such values.
- The person has the ability to execute the implementation of moral actions, involving behaviour that is consistent with the realisation of one's goals (Conger 1991: 466–467).

2.4.2 Factors influencing the adolescent's morals

2.4.2.1 Parental influence

The adolescent learns what is regarded as right and what is regarded as wrong from his parents. Adults interpret for him the moral codes of the community and punish him when he violates them. Once parents believe that the adolescent has already learned the major principles of right and wrong, they will frequently neglect to teach him the relationship between the specific principle learned earlier and the general principles that are essential for control over behaviour in adult life.

The fact that parents assume adolescents know what is right explains their tendency to punish what they regard as intentional misbehaviour (Mathunyane 1992: 45; Hurlock 1973: 248; and Hurlock 1980: 243).

2.4.2.1 Sexual roles

Girls' acceptance of parental standards assumes different forms in early and late adolescence. Younger girls accept parental direction unselfconsciously, seldom questioning its correctness; whereas older ones offer reasons for identifying with their parents' point of view. Older girls may assume in fantasy the role of mother and seek to justify views that they will soon be required to defend.

Boys progress towards moral maturity with uncertainty. They criticise moral dilemmas they meet, often questioning and testing the limits. They may ultimately arrive at the same conclusion that many girls adopted earlier. It could be argued that each sex develops according to the moral patterns best suited for its future role of mother or father (Mathunyane 1992: 46)

2.4.2.3 Peer group conformity

Adolescents' views are strongly modified by those of their peers. The unstructured free hours spent with peers affords them the opportunity to develop role-playing skills. Time spent with peers involves egalitarian relationships and shared interests, which are more rewarding than task- orientated hierarchical relationships with their middle-aged parents. The differences in lifestyle between parents and adolescent peers cause them to interpret the morality of behaviours from different perspectives (Rogers 1985: 169).

2.4.2. 4 Moral values from a traditional African perspective

The members of the African society believe that their moral values were given to them by God. They further believe that some of the departed ones keep watch over the living to make sure that they observe moral laws and to punish them when they break them. With regard to sexual ethics among the traditional nations, boys and girls are expected to enjoy sexual experiences after puberty and the completion of relevant lessons. Among other traditional nations, girls receive sex education and are also coached on how to behave towards men during and after puberty. Mothers also play a role in the choice of a spouse (Harries 1929: 53; Kuper 1986: 53–54).

2.4.2. 5 The educational process in the life world of a traditional African child

Tribes men

Rituals performed are part of the educative process, a symbolic affirmation of certain social values. Formal education is given in the initiation schools, which play a very important part in the life of every individual.

Menstruation and erotic dreams are, amongst others, some of the signs that indicate that the child is biologically ready for sex. Many traditional parents do not discuss intercourse, contraception, abortion, menstruation, or erotic dreams with their children. Children receive sexual instructions in the initiation schools. Boys and girls are separated and isolated, taught, and circumcised. They will be kept in seclusion until they finish their course.

The *koma/ingoma* (initiation school) is under the guidance of the principal teacher, who accounts to the chief. The principal teacher (*rabadiya*) is a man of harsh temperament, daring, and a skilled hunter. The school aims at vesting in the *amakwenkwe* (initiates) the powers and privileges of full participation in the social and political activities in the adult world.

The initiates are brought into direct contact with the history, law, customs, and philosophy of the tribe. The past is put before them, and they get acquainted with the magical powers emanating from ancestral spirits (*amadlozi*). The initiates are taught that the spirits of the ancestors live on and determine the fortunes and mishaps of the individual and the tribe and that through him (the initiate), the gods must be preserved and be perpetuated.

The content in the syllabus covers areas like:

- The necessity of obeying, respecting, and keeping the confidence of his chief is impressed upon the boy (*mutukana*).
- Obedience to his father is emphasised.
- Guidance for self-control and respect for all men and women, is offered.
- They are prepared for marriage and for public duties of the adult status.
- Courage and endurance are instilled. As a result, when the circumcision operation is carried out, the boy stoically cooperates with the *inchibi* (the operator). His emotional sentiment is calmed by saying, 'Monna ke nku, o llela teng.' This means 'a man is like a sheep, he does not cry out loud'. Henceforth, for every ordeal,

he is forced to undergo a severe test of endurance (Pitje 1950: 121–122; Lekhela 1958: 23–25; Raum 1967: 100; and Harries 1929: 69–70).

In some ethnic groups, a girl (*musidzana*) also attends an initiation school (*vhusha*) under the direction of the principal wife of the chief. Girls are taught about marriage, parenting, and sexuality. They are strictly advised to respect all men and, in particular, the chief.

In a multicultural society, the traditional practices and beliefs of the Africans are more often than not challenged by the introduction of the Western formal education system.

In this system, there are no separate schools for traditional and Western- oriented African children. All the schools impart similar value orientations. In this scenario, the African child finds himself between two sources of command, namely, home and the school. On the one hand, parents expect children to retain their home identity, and on the other hand, the school explicitly or implicitly encourages conformity to school life (Disasa 1988: 17).

concrete building

Traditional house

2.5 Synthesis

Man acquired the mortality status by violating God's instructions. In order to save the world, God showed his mercy and love by sending his only Son, Jesus Christ, to reveal immortality by ending the power of death.

Only human beings can differentiate between right and wrong and are the only beings that exist in relation to God, self, and other people. Religion and moral education are partners in nurturing man towards a blessed destination.

The next chapter will deal with leadership within democracy.

CHAPTER 3

LEADERSHIP WITHIN DEMOCRACY

I have cherished the ideal of a democratic and free society in which all persons live together in harmony and with equal opportunities.

Nelson Mandela

Subjects

3.1 The establishment of governance structures
3.2 Democracy
3.3 Role players in democracy
3.4 Leadership
3.5 Educational implications for teaching and learning within a democracy
3.6 Synthesis

> **Keywords**
>
> *leadership, democracy, equality, learner council, civil society, state, desalinate, intellect, personality, servant-leader, recreational leader, school climate, school culture, educational induction*

3.1 The establishment of governance structures

Flags of various nations   Meeting congress

God said to man, 'Be fruitful and multiply, fill the earth and govern it.' This injunction serves as a delegation of duties for man to govern this one big family, which is fragmented into various groups, communities, and societies.

The wickedness of man compelled God to impose laws enforcing the respect of human life and harmonious relationships. In order to promote good order, the establishment of governance structures became imperative. In establishing a government (Zechariah 6:11–14), 'God put a crown on the head of the High Priest and said, the man who is called the Branch will flourish where he is. He is the one who will build the Lord's Temple and receive the honour due to a King and He will rule his people. A Priest will stand by his throne; the King and the Priest will work together in peace and harmony; and God will rule completely over all' (1 Corinthians 15:28).

Therefore, in the promotion of social cohesion, the *government* worked together with *churches* and received authority, power, and wisdom from God. The command was that everyone must obey the state and authorities because no authority exists without God's permission (Romans 13:1–7).

There are also systems in place that govern the behaviour of those in power or authority. These may be called the church or state constitutions. Concepts like democracy, equality, and freedom dominate almost all constitutions.

3.2 Democracy

Christian democracy stands on the belief that all persons are equal before the Heavenly Father, and it recognises the divinity of Christ and the brotherly love taught and exemplified by Jesus (Redden and Ryan 1956: 584).

The conviction of civil society is that all persons are equal in origin, nature, and purpose. Majority rule is the norm, with the proviso that such a rule brings peace and political, social, and economic development to be enjoyed by all.

The founding principle of majority rule is that of equality, to be equal before the law.

Equality means to be equal before the law and the right to equal protection and benefits of the law. It includes the full and equal enjoyment of all rights and freedom (Constitution of the Republic of South Africa 1996).

Helen Suzman, the leader of the opposition party in South Africa (1961 to 1974) always maintained that the indispensible elements in a democratic society are simple justice, equal opportunity, and human rights and that these are worth fighting for (Sheldon 2005: 238).

Democracy protects and balances the freedom of one against the freedom of another. A democratic leader is a servant of all and always acts in the best interest of all.

God works through the Holy Spirit to rule the hearts of all and, through civil governance, to order common life; that is, God reigns in both spiritual and temporal authorities (LSB 2009: 1579).

True democracy acknowledges that the dignity and worth of an individual are based on:

- divine creation
- moral nature
- inalienable rights
- his final end in God.

On the whole, law regulates over the exercise of freedom and liberty. Consciousness is the greatest element of coexistence.

3.3 Role players in democracy

3.3.1 Church organisations, civil society, and the state

The church is the light and salt of the world (Matthew 5:13–14). Salt is a purification, preservation, and flavouring agent. Light symbolises knowledge. The implications are that the church is the custodian of all good things and should be seen taking its rightful position in salting and enlightening.

Respect between the two institutions—namely, the church and government—has to be reciprocal. The church must refrain from working hand in glove with the state because this carries a risk of its saltiness diminishing. If the church gets into the pocket of the state, it will at some stage remain silent when it should be speaking out against unrighteousness.

On the other hand, it is detrimental for the church to be isolated or to play a passive role in civil and state activities. Non-participation may render the church redundant; it will lose its saltiness, and its light may go off *forever*. Therefore, it is important and right for believers/Christians to participate actively in all spheres of life (Keeley 1982: 441).

3.3.2 The responsibilities of civilians and Christians towards the state

Brother James, my fellow Christian and the execute mayor of our town, has the duty to care faithfully for the electorate and render services accordingly as the law stipulates. The Holy Spirit fully supports civil (his) authority.

The responsibilities of civilians are:

- to honour and respect authorities at all times
- to obey the laws of the country
- to practise love
- to be compliant—that is, to pay taxes—because the authorities are working for God when they fulfil their duties
- to pay personal and property taxes (Romans 13:6–7)
- to submit to rulers and authorities (Titus 3:1).

3.4 Leadership

> WHEREVER THERE ARE LOCAL LEADERS, THEIR ORDERS SHOULD BE OBEYED BY THE PEOPLE.
>
> Mohandas K. (Mahatma) Gandhi

3.4.1 The empowered leader

Government as a big structure is divided into departments or ministries, which are manned by men and women who account to the head of the state. To maintain successful state machinery, these men and women, in their various portfolios, need to be allocated working tools, human and physical resources, and finances for empowerment purposes.

All these must be coupled with appropriate academic qualifications, good intellectual and personality traits, as well as appropriate experience. It is also expected of these leaders to act and behave according to certain general, moral, and social standards and to use their power and authority for the benefit of all.

A leader is someone who holds a particular office (namely, the director general, the chief financial officer, and so on) and may also be someone with the highest level of skills for a particular task (Prinsloo et al. 1994: 102).

Leadership is explained and described in various ways, namely:

- Leadership is the capacity to complete a task with the assistance of others, at the same time winning their respect, loyalty, and cooperation.
- Leadership is a process whereby one individual influences other group members towards the attainment of defined goals.
- Leadership contains two important components, namely, authority and power.
- √ Authority has to do with the right of a manager/administrator to enforce certain actions within specific guidelines and the right to take action against those who will not cooperate.
- √ Power is the ability to influence the behaviour of others, the ability to influence followers and exercise authority effectively (compare Plunkett (1975); Gerber et al. 1998: 229; Bergh et al. 1999: 224).

3.4.2 Effective leaders

The changing world demands leaders to be versatile and prepared to face the challenges that come as a result of developments in the social, political, economic, and cultural fronts. Amidst all these, the courage to implement new ideas and tackling new tasks are signs of growth and development. Leadership is all about risk-taking.

3.4.2.1 The innate characteristics of leaders

Leaders are born with innate characteristics that enable them to influence others, and these are:

- intellectual characteristics: decisiveness, judgemental ability, knowledge, and verbal abilities
- personality characteristics:
  - ➤ extraversion: sociable, talkative, assertive
  - ➤ emotional stability: good-natured, cooperative, trusting, calm, and enthusiastic
  - ➤ conscientiousness: careful, thorough, responsible, achievement oriented, and persevering
  - ➤ openness: imaginative, cultural, curious, original, broad-minded, and artistically sensitive
- physicalcharacteristics: presentable (Dipboye et al. 1994; Ivancevich et al. 1993).

Leaders generally must be:

- knowledgeable, decisive, judgemental, and have verbal abilities
- aware of group members' talents, skills, and their attitudes to one another and to their assignments
- concerned about the conditions in which the group has to function
- aware of available resources
- constantly evaluating the changing circumstances within the group and effecting improvements where necessary (Napoli et al. 1988: 224).

3.4.2.2 Qualities portraying the true image of a servant-leader

A servant-leader is a follower and imitator of Christ. He is expected to give leadership by serving in harmony and peace.

The following are few examples of a servant-leader:

- He or she is a person of prayer. 'We prayed for God to protect us, and he answered our prayers' (Ezra 8:23).
- He or she is a humble person. 'Please sir, accept this present, please forgive me sir, for any wrong I have done' (1 Samuel 25:27–28).
- He or she is a selflessness/unselfish person. Abigail takes the blame for the actions of Nabal (1 Samuel 25:24).
- He or she is a person of discipline, self-control, knowledge and love. 'Do your best to add goodness to your faith; to your goodness add knowledge; to your knowledge add self-control; to your self-control add endurance; to your endurance add godliness; to your godliness add brotherly affection; and to your brotherly affection add love. (2 Peter 1:5–7).
- He or she is a faithful/trustworthy/dependable person. 'In all he does, he is faithful and just; all his commands are dependable. They last for all time; they were given in truth and righteousness' (Psalm 111: 7–8).
- He or she is a loyal person. 'Oh Lord, I will always sing for your constant love, I will proclaim your faithfulness' (Psalm 89:1).
- He or she is a caring and sacrificing person. 'Tabitha the believer, spent all her time doing good and helping the poor' (Acts 9:36).
- He or she is a person who appreciates with thanks. 'It is Christ who lives in me. This life that I live now, I live by faith in the Son of God, who loved me and

gave his life for me' (Galatians 2:20). 'And I am filled with thanksgiving' (Colossians 2:7).
- He or she is a truthful person. 'Lead them to the truth taught by our religion. God who does not lie, promised us this life before the beginning of time' (Titus 1:1–2).
- He or she is a diligent, patient, and a sharing person. 'Well done, you good and faithful servant, come in and share my happiness' (Matthew 25:21, 23). 'I waited patiently for the Lord's help, then he listened to me and heard my cry' (Psalm 40:1).
- He or she is a persevering and an enduring person. 'Whoever holds out to the end, will be saved' (Matthew 24:13).

3.4.2.3 The recreational leader

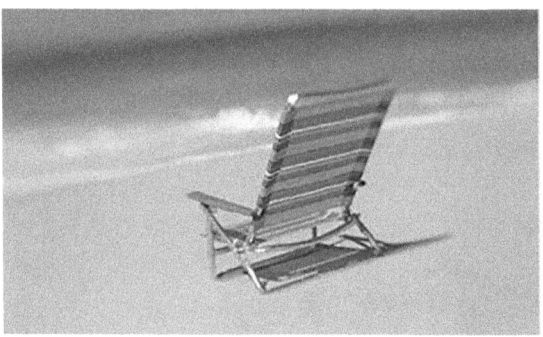

Beach chair

There is one aspect related to the productivity of the worker/servant that is to be taken seriously: God completed his creation in six days, and on the seventh day, he rested (Genesis 2:2). This implies that a hard-working servant of God, in the shepherding of his flock, has also to enjoy leisure time. Put differently, this means that work and toil without recreation breeds laziness and unproductiveness, all of which will affect the worker's general output.

Leisure is equated to free time. Free time implies that if a person is not working, then he is at leisure.

Leisure benefits the worker in the following ways:

- It relaxes the individual.
- It entertains the person.
- It promotes personal development of the individual through his voluntary participation in social and cultural life (Gerdes et al. 1981: 250).

> She walks—the lady of my delight—A shepherdess of sheep. Her flock are thoughts—she keeps them white; she guards them from the steep. She feeds them on the fragrant height, And folds them in for sleep.
>
> Alice Meynell
> **The shepherdess**

3.5 Educational implications for teaching and learning within a Democracy

Teacher and pupils discussion

3.5.1 The establishment of a positive educational climate in a democratic school environment

According to Van Deventer and Kruger (2003: 14–17), 'school climate is the quality and frequency of interaction between all the stakeholders involved in the school. School culture, is the belief system or values of those stakeholders. Therefore, the school climate may be seen as those interactions that underpin the school culture, which includes typical patterns of activities that are characteristics of the functioning of a particular school'.

Caring, is a typical characteristic of a teacher–learner relationship. Schools that care encourage children to participate meaningfully and to perform to the best of their abilities.

In order to achieve maturity, the learner needs adult support. He has to enter into relationships with supportive adults. Nicholls et al. (1983: 22) point to the fact that a teacher is a person with above-average academic ability and that the teacher's experience can be used for the benefit of the learners. The teacher needs to be able to communicate and work with others towards the development of skills in learners.

In a learning opportunity, learners prefer a learning context which arouses a feeling of independence and a sense of responsibility for getting the work done. A learner enjoys being given the opportunity to tell his classmates what he has found out about a given topic and discuss it with them. The teacher in this type of arrangement should appear as a figure with whom learners may discuss their work and who offers suggestions and encourages enquiry and questioning. In such a case, a teacher gives learners greater responsibility for their own learning and allows them to exercise judgement and to make some choices in relation to their learning (Nicholls et al. 1983: 61; Cole and Halll 1970: 586).

Sound relationships between teachers and learners contribute to the creation of an educational environment that is supportive to learning. These relationships encourage a freedom of questioning, understanding, and independent thinking. The learner is greatly empowered and is in a position to:

- know his teacher in such a way that his language and body language are explicitly interpreted
- understand the teacher's sense of humour.

And on the other hand, the teacher will treat the learners with respect, and all efforts will be made to convert the classroom into a small community or social units that resembles what is taking place in the bigger community.

3.5.2 Educational induction into society

According to Johnson (1968: 110), socialisation is learning that enables the learner to perform social roles. The educational and social situations and relations are intertwined social aspects (Gunter 1977: 27).

In high schools, children have several classes, and each class has a structure of its own since the individuals composing it are different. The learners in the class group form various relationships, and it is much easier to notice their social behaviour.

The extracurricular activities are implemented by the school for purposes of accommodating the child in activities outside the classroom. Learners' activities may include sports, social events (like parties and dances), dramatics, speech festivals, clubs, and learner representative councils. All these activities share a common goal, that of making children worthy citizens in their communities (Bent 1970: 376).

Learners' interests in these activities should be fully cultivated in order to realise the desired educational goals.

- Drama (acting)—acting is encouraged in order to promote sound character formation. Drama may prove a source of great pleasure to children (Sadler 1948: 268).
- Learner councils—high schools may have a student government that operates through the student council. Through this activity, the learners practise techniques of government and learn how voting is done, how laws are formulated and passed, and how rules are enforced. These activities give practical training in citizenship (Cole and Hall 1970: 566).
- Sport activities—the high school places a high value on sport activities. Athletics, soccer, and rugby teams provide a basis for much of the social life of the child. Participation in sport teams may be the primary force which motivates the child to remain in school. For other participants, sports add dimensions to their lives which enhance personal and social development (Lerner and Spanier 1980: 48).
- Clubs and special groups—a large number of clubs and special groups contribute enormously to the socialisation of high school learners. Language and literary (debating) societies, public speaking, and many others make the school an attractive place (Sadler 1948: 269) and prepares learners to take their leadership roles in society.

Extracurricular school activities are, however, only a part of the total school experience, and the total school experience is only a part of the total life and growth experience of the child; therefore, all the dynamics or activities contribute towards growth and maturity (Sybouts and Krepel 1984: 61).

3.5.3 The role of leadership in school excellence

No learning organisation can achieve excellence without the *commitment* of the school leadership. The principal has to set standards and expectations for the school community. It is a matter of necessity that she/he raises the bar that will stimulate excellence (Moloi 2002: 89; Budhal 2000: 18).

The school's leadership/principal must become the custodian of the teaching time. He must see to it that more work is put in the hour, not more hours in the work, and therefore, strategic initiatives that will encourage and inspire effective learning have to be developed.

The school management team, the teaching staff, and the administrative personnel have to be involved in the planning, management, and supervision of the school activities.

This involvement evokes a feeling of belonging and ownership, and thus all energies will be harnessed towards the achievement of excellence.

3.6 Synthesis

Leaders on earth are appointed by God. Knowledge, intellect, personality traits, life skills, and above all, power and authority have been given to man to manage the world.

A true servant-leader is empowered to face the challenges that prevail in the societal, religious, political, economical fronts. All risks taken in an attempt to build a nation must at least meet the minimum requirements of working towards a peaceful, orderly, and result-driven organisation.

The next chapter will deal with the life theatre.

CHAPTER 4

THE LIFE THEATRE

African tribal designs

> I am an African.
>
> I am born of the peoples of the continent of Africa.
>
> I owe my being to the hills and the valleys, the mountains and the glades, the rivers, the deserts, the trees, the flowers, the seas and the ever changing seasons that define the face of our native land.
>
> We could be both at home and be foreign, and human existence demands that freedom is a necessary condition for human existence.
>
> Thabo Mbeki

Subjects

4.1 Arts and worship
4.2 Religious, traditional rituals, and healing
4.3 Sports: The international language
4.4 The driver of life: Life skills
4.5 The educational implications for learning and teaching within the theatrical life world
4.6 Synthesis

> **Keywords**
>
> *amadlozi, amathonga, arts, badimo, worship, idolatry, healing ministry, spiritual and faith healing, consciousness, o tsenwe ke moya, dreams, psychic divination, ancestral spirits, Christian healing, drugs, hallucinogens, hlogwana, tropo, letshollo, life skills, uhudo*

4.1 Arts and worship

Art in most instances is associated with *religion*. The two are associated because a human being is a religious being and there is therefore always a need for him to worship.

Man believes that God expresses himself in many ways, such as in material things that display the product of his hands through artwork, and this work boosts the power of imagination and deepens the appreciation of what it is to be human.

Also man maintains that all creation stands in relation to the Creator and all people of earth must therefore worship and honour the Lord (Psalms 33:6–8).

Art and idolatry more often go together. Idolatry is a situation where man regards something material or natural as having power and deserving of worship. This includes the love of animals, things, a piece of wood, gold, silver, etc., which are man-made (formed by human hands).

> They have mouths but cannot speak.
> They have eyes but cannot see.
> They have ears but cannot hear.
> They have noses but cannot smell.
> They have hands but cannot feel.
> They have feet but cannot walk.
> And they cannot make a sound. (Psalms 115:4–8)

But man seeks help and consolation from these creatures, thus placing trust in anything that is not God (LSB 2009: 1370).

Idolatry is a sensitive, complicated aspect of life, varies from religion to religion, and needs to be handled with great care.

The love for money and the desire to have more and more of it is idolatry and nothing else (Keeley 1982: 253).

Other religions have a variety of gods, for example:

- the god of money and possessions (the whole trust is put on money and property)
- the god of wisdom, education, power, and prestige
- the god of need (I have a toothache, and therefore, I must fast in the honour of St Mathews!)
- the god of fear (there is a threatening pandemic in our community; therefore, I must make a vow to St Abraham or St Peter)
- the god in partnership I have an agreement with my god so that he may help me in love affairs, protect my livestock, recover my lost TV set, etc.)
- my own god (I am looking for blessings, happiness, and comfort; Tom may set up his own god, e.g. moon, for riches and pleasure, while Henry may set up his own god, e.g. Venus, for riches and pleasure).
- my wife is pregnant (therefore, she will worship St Lucia (Tappert et al. 1959: 367)).

The purpose of the commandment 'worship no god but me' is to make people understand that there is only one God and no other; it is a commandment that gives true faith and confidence of the heart and impresses upon man to look upon God alone. If your *faith* and *trust* are pure, then your god is a living god. To look to God implies that whatever good thing you lack, seek it from God; whenever you suffer misfortunes and distress, look to God (Tappert et al. 1959: 365).

Look further on our daily activities in the community as well as in church; there are certain human traditional rites which are performed from time to time. Too often they degenerate to the level of being a god rather than enhancing the worshipping of God.

The reasons why some traditional rites have to be observed are:

- Rites enhance the teaching and preaching of the Word of God.
- Rites promote tranquillity and order.
- They are beneficial in that they give people a sense of time and how to do things decently.

But be reminded that the observance of these rites has no bearing to the forgiveness of sins and have nothing to do with helping an individual in gaining grace (Tappert et al. 1959: 215–221).

4.2 Religious and traditional rituals and healing

4.2.1 The healing ministry

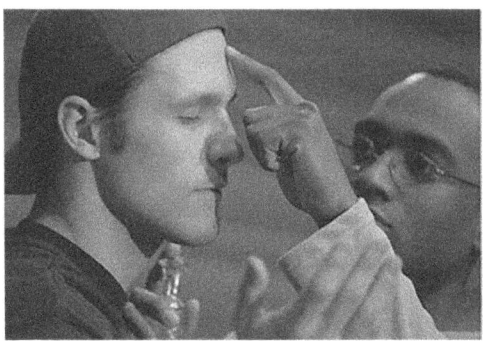

Jesus was teaching, preaching, and healing people who had all kinds of diseases (Matthew 4:23), and in the same spirit, he commissioned his followers to go and preach and heal people. This inspired true Christians to devote special days for prayer sessions for the sick (Keeley 1982: 388).

Various churches use different ways in their healing ministry. Some use the laying of hands, and others use the anointing of oil and so on; this comes as an implementation of the directive in James 5:14–15, which says, 'If there is anyone who is ill; He should send for the church elders who will pray for him and rub olive oil on him in the name of the Lord. This prayer made in faith will heal the sick person; the Lord will restore him to good health.'

4.2.2 Spiritual or faith healing

The focal point of spiritual or faith healing is the willpower of an individual. This person will be named the prophet or apostle. The belief in them is so intense that non-compliance to instructions translates to a curse. Instructions like eating cow dung, rats, snakes and drinking paraffin are complied with—without questions.

Singing and dancing are part and parcel of spiritual rituals/practices and play a role in consciousness. Consciousness refers to all the thoughts, sensations, and emotions of what a person is aware of at any given moment (Louw and Edwards 1993: 173).

In most instances, music, singing, and dancing evoke emotions like love, devotion, humility, tenderness, and so forth. During this time, when your spirits are high, you're everyday thinking is converted, and the person singing and dancing gets deeply involved and enters in the altered state of consciousness—*o tsenwe ke moya* (he has been possessed by the spirits). The songs and verses repeated in the process converts the singers' personal interests and encourage the spirit to talk and give some revelations.

The altered state of consciousness differs from one individual to another. Martindale and Smith (Louw and Edwards 1993: 174) give a perceived view of the consequences of the altered state of consciousness:

- The perceptual process is disturbed (hearing or feeling something that does not exist).
- Cognitive processes may become superficial and undiscriminating.
- Normal inhibitions and self-control can weaken.
- Memory disorders can occur.

The whole process encompasses psychic divination, and that is how ancestral spirits express themselves. Dreams and visions experienced (at any time) are a prominent feature of psychic divination.

Dreams commonly occur throughout sleep and fulfil unconscious wishes, which appear in a disguised way, and in most episodes, the dreams are unpleasant (Passer et al. 2001: 189–192). Daydreaming is an altered state of consciousness, regarded as an alternative reality, and features as a unique characteristic of human consciousness (Louw and Edwards 1993: 175).

The merit and demerits of daydreaming are explained as follows:

- It serves as a practice session in anticipation of future actions.
- It is a source of creative thinking for writers and inventors.
- It is a notion of hope or fear beyond the sober limit of probability.

4.2.3 Christian healing

The omniscient Lord has created medical science, and therefore, the health sciences and professional health workers have been placed at our disposal for use as part of Christian healing.

The omnipresence of Jesus Christ gives all believers *faith and hope* that with the use of medicine, together with prayers and intercessions, the sick will get well. Prayer is medicine, and the use of medicine without faith and hope is a futile exercise. Christian healing is not confined to physical sickness but goes beyond and prays for the whole person, relationships, attitudes, and emotions. Through faith in Christ, Christians accept the fact that one may not get healed at the time of prayer, but Christians will continue to pray in church, at their homes, and also pay home or hospital visits for prayer and moral support. Take your medicine with a faithful prayer. This is Christian healing.

4.2.4 The use of drugs in religious and traditional healing

The use of drugs plays a role in the state of consciousness. Drugs like aspirin and/or paracetamol have minor effects on consciousness. Drugs like hallucinogens or psychedelics—for example, lysergic acid diethylamide (LSD)—distorts or intensifies sensory experiences, evokes hallucinations and disordered thought processes, and produces dramatic and unusual experiences (Louw and Edwards 1993: 187; Passer et al. 2001: 200).

Drugs have been used to activate intense spiritual experiences. There are many medicinal plants which are used as psychedelics drugs. Some churches combine Christian elements with the use of drugs, alcohol, plants, and roots to produce medicine. Traditional healers also use medicinal plants—namely, tree leaves, barks, and roots—as their traditional medicine.

4.2.5 The relationship between traditional medicine and Western biotechnology

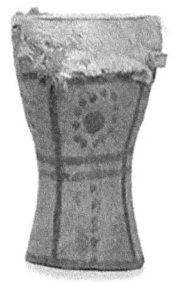
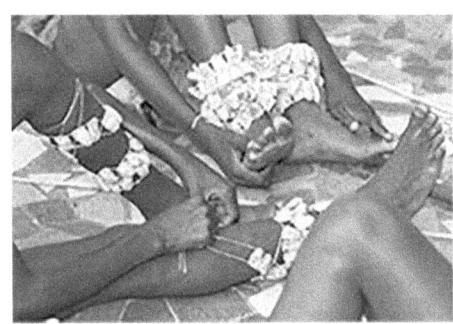

The African drum   African dancers

Felhaber and Mayeng (Masoga and Musyoki 2001: 51) explain indigenous or traditional healing as encompassing the following order of processes:

- observation—looking for the symptoms of the disease
- patient self-diagnosis—patient relating the symptoms
- divination—this involves bone-throwing: ditaola/ukubhula (afri- urban lingo= floor X- ray), evoking ancestral spirits, psyche, dreams, and visions; this method of healing strongly portrays the power and processes of ancestral spirits.

The ancestral spirits (*badimo* or *amadlozi* or *amathonga*) are personalised gods. When a person dies, the spirit departs and leaves the body and continues to exist as a single entity. The ancestors are believed to have survived death and to be living in a spiritual world. They become the guardians of the earth. They see and hear everything and take a lively interest in all the affairs of their families, their health, and fertility. Given the fact that they are elders, they will also seek rebirth into the family. They also wish to be remembered at all times. The badimo have full access to the channels of communicating with God directly or through their own forefathers (Parrinder 1954: 58–59; Smith 1950: 85; Mbiti 1971 83).

In order to become a Sangoma or herbalist, the power of the ancestral spirit must evoke a relevant behavior in the form of Ancestral dreams and psychiatric problems.

A person possessed by ancestral spirits will demonstrate uncontrollable crying and sweating and thereafter, start speaking softly, indicating who that ancestor is, who died many years ago, calling him/her to this service.

The approach in the traditional diagnosis of the disease and its treatment runs parallel with the approach used in the Western system. For example, on the one hand, bone-throwing is used and the ancestral spirits mystically reveal the medicine to be used. On the other hand, deceases are properly listed, and the treatment thereof is well documented and/or prescribed. Diagnosis is determined by the use of technology.

THE DICHOTOMY: FACTS AND PERCEPTIONS

For a deeper understanding of the two systems, this can be demonstrated by giving the following illustration:

Herbal medicine

Female Nurse

Table 2 Comparison of the traditional and Western medicine

Name of disease	Signs and symptoms	Traditional treatment	Western therapy
Hlogwana	This is the sinking crown of the infant's head	A powder mixture of a burnt animal skull and an herb is applied in the incision made on the head.	Fontanel: This is the soft area between the bones of the skull (cranium) in an infant. During birth, the baby's head through the birth canal is 'moulded' temporarily out of shape. The rigid fusion of the bones in the infant's skull is delayed and will take shape naturally and stop moving in a few months.

Tropo (discharge)	This is sexually transmitted infection (STI)	A mixture of herbs poured into a two-litre container is taken every day until the infection is cleared.	Gonorrhoea: it is treated by antibiotic medications.
Letshollo, uhudo	This is excessive diarrhoea that may lead to blood discharge	The powder of a mixture of herbs (similar to a crushed charcoal) is given to the sick person to lick until the diarrhoea stops.	Diarrhoea: Generally, the patient loses fluid and body chemicals. In severe cases, the patient is admitted in the hospital, and the lost fluid and body chemicals are replaced intravenously. Antidiarrhoeal agents are also given to stabilise the stomach.
Mental lllness	Schezophrenic symptoms- Physical and Psychological problems. I rratability, aggression and social withdrawal	Healing will take place within the context of religion; because sickness is regarded as a religious matter. Symptoms tell you that this person has a spiritual problem. These are signs to show that the patient has a calling towards a healing profession. The cure, is to become a traditional healer/sangoma.	Clinical procedures and the therapy will be based on the Diagnostic and Statistical Manual of Mental Disorders.

(CompareShryock 1983:29,47O,536-537;Masoga and Musyoki 2001: 53 - 59).

THE DICHOTOMY: FACTS AND PERCEPTIONS

Traditional medicine and the method of healing are perceived as incomparable and far-fetched from the clinical procedures of Western medicine. Some Western therapists view African beliefs as primitive, unhealthy, and superstitious (Jane Mufamadi in Masoga and Musyoki 2001: 59). This attitude and lack of understanding on these aspects may result in the *polarisation of relationships*.

Magwa, Cooposamy, and Mayekiso (Masoga and Musyoki 2001: 49–50) elaborate extensively on the comparative relationships of indigenous plant usage and Western biotechnology methods:

- *Peppermint oil* (indigenous to the United States of America) and scotch spearmint are used to flavour chewing gum, candy, toothpaste, and medicine.
- The wild South African indigenous *rooibos tea* is known for its aroma and its low tannin content. It has high level of minerals and free radical–capturing properties.
- Lippia javanica is a South African medicinal plant for treating arthritis, rheumatism, and high blood pressure.
- *Aloe vera* is an excellent traditional medicine and has superior healing powers. Today, it is in demand and dominates the pharmaceutical and cosmetic industries.
- Almost all these *traditional medicines* are now popular and are extensively and/or intensively used in modern Western medicine.

Scientists, health practitioners (Western), and traditional practitioners agree that much collaboration between the indigenous and Western therapists is extremely desired and long overdue. This will advantage all people and, in particular, those in the areas where access to Western medical care is not affordable or accessible. The desired collaboration will develop and encourage respect and the integrity of both approaches.

4.3 Sports: The international language

Sports have been labelled the only universal language. This implies that sports accommodate diversity. Players in the sports field gain external physical fitness, a sense of well-being, and friends. For those on the grandstand, whether some are from the west or east, the excitement and enjoyment is enormous, and relationships are formed; rivals smile and hug one another.

The spectators and or supporters are given an opportunity to be part of the whole crowd or supporters' clubs, sharing victory or loss, developing sportsmanship, accepting defeat, and celebrating victory.

On the whole, children and adults place a high value in sporting activities. Sports in general provide enjoyment, fun, and discipline and are regarded as the basis for personal and social development for all as well as an agent of social cohesion.

4.4 The driver of life: Life skills

Life skills are abilities for adaptive and positive behaviour that enables one to deal effectively with the demands and challenges of everyday life (WHO 1993).

Hutchinson (1992: 180, 828) expands this and says life skills can be seen as 'coping tools' to survive every day's emotional, social, and cognitive onslaughts. *Cope* and *tools* are explained in the following manner:

- *Cope* is 'the ability to deal effectively with a challenge'.
- *Tool* is 'an implement that gives the user an advantage over a person who does not have such a tool'.

The Lord has provided a helper, namely the *Holy Spirit*. The Holy Spirit gives guidance and impresses upon all that everything and the strengths to face all conditions is by the power of Christ (Philippians 4:13).

The above exposition literally describes life skills as tools a person should be equipped with in order to have insight into life tasks and manage them successfully (Landsberg 2005: 97).

Engelbrecht et al. (1996: 285–286) support the view that there is a core set of life skills for the promotion of the health and well-being of children and adults; and these are:

- Decision-making skills help in making well-informed and meaningful and feasible decisions.
- Problem-solving skills help one to deal decisively with problems.
- Creative-thinking skills helps with the evaluation, analysing, choosing between alternatives and to stick to choices made, irrespective of consequences.
- Critical-thinking skills help one to analyse information and experiences objectively.
- Effective communication skills help one to articulate oneself clearly.
- Interpersonal relationship skills help one to relate passionately with others.
- Self-awareness involves the individual's awareness of his strength and weaknesses as well as his character.
- Empathy is the ability to express empathy for another person, and this helps one to accept others who may be different.
- Coping with stress is the ability to relax and to keep cool and calm.

There is a life skill which is, above all, given as a heavenly gift. 'God so loved the world that He gave his only Son so that everyone who believes in Him may not perish, but may have eternal life' (John 3:16). Prayer is the appropriate tool to use in order to nurture and sustain your belief as well as to open the doors of heaven. Equally, children are given a holy life skill, that of respecting their parents. By so doing, all will go well with them, and they will live a long time on earth.

4.5 The educational implications for learning and teaching within the theatrical life world

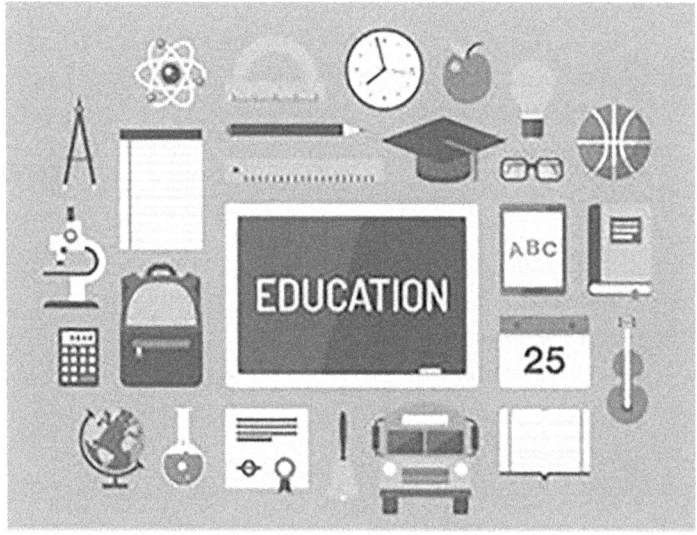

The education provided to Christian children consists of elements such as faith, which is based on the individual's belief and practices on religious observances in common with others on the same faith. The Christian teaching revolves around a way of life to be lived and a work of authority and love. The teacher—by exemplifying his own life, the way of life taught by Christ—contribute positively in shaping children's behaviour and attitude towards education.

The school environment includes all experiences with which children come into contact—namely, physical structure, content material, learning process, and the staff members of the school. Fullan (1997: 42) avers that for education or teaching and learning to be effective, the teacher must be a good role model. If so, learners will succeed. If learners succeed and excel, the society will develop. The classroom environment that is orderly and aesthetically pleasing has a positive effect on the child's learning. According to Rutter (Collins 1984: 288), there is a positive relationship between decoration and care of the building and children's development.

The inclusion of music and singing in the curriculum is equal to providing water to a thirsty soul and nurturing the spiritual, moral, and emotional aspects of life. Music and dancing are powerful worshipping tools (Mathunyane 2015:67). These remain indispensable in that:

- Messages are best communicated to the heart through music than in any other way.
- Music is healing.
- Music enables people to relax.
- Music enables people for serious meditation on the gospel message.
- Music and singing comforts the sick, bereaved, weak in spirit, and depressed. The involvement of parents in the school sporting activities has a bearing on the children's attitude towards sports, behaviour, level of performance, and enjoyment. Positive encouragement from teachers, parents, and fans (members of the community) contribute to the following aspects in children:self- esteem
- sense of personal achievement and satisfaction
- enjoyment of the sport
- social development
- physical fitness
- respect for rules and regulations
- respect for other people's differences.

THE DICHOTOMY: FACTS AND PERCEPTIONS

Parents and teachers who give children the opportunity to learn a variety of skills enable them to make significant choices and to take responsibility for their actions.

The school has the responsibility of encouraging learning by:

- ➤ helping children to identify their skills and abilities
- ➤ directing them to develop self-control.

Life skills in totality have to take centre stage and have to be used in educational programmes in the following areas:

 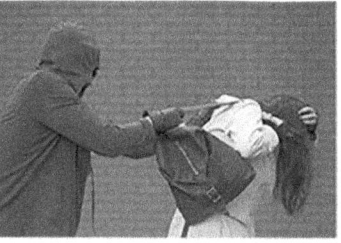

Adolescents drinking and smoking   A girl in danger

prevention of substance abuse since violence in and around schools is often associated with alcohol and drug abuse

- ➤ teenage pregnancy, awareness of the consequences of unsafe and unprotected sex (for example, pregnancy, sexually transmitted infections, HIV, and AIDS)
- ➤ promotion of cognitive, emotional, and affective development
- ➤ promotion of health and social developmental tasks—namely, prevention of bullying, teaching people about peace, education on prevention and treatment of AIDS
- ➤ promotion of self-confidence and self-esteem.

4.6 Synthesis

A human being is a religious being, and therefore, there is always a need to worship. God reveals to man that an idol is a piece of wood, gold, or silver which is man-made and therefore cannot be God. The purpose of the commandment 'worship no God but me' is to impress upon man to look upon God alone.

Arts, sports, culture, drugs, music, and singing are the embellishers of the life spectacle.

Life skills enable all to deal with the demands and challenges of everyday life. Amongst many, there is one life skill which is full of blessings— namely, to respect parents and all people.

The next chapter will deal with social development.

THE DICHOTOMY: FACTS AND PERCEPTIONS

CHAPTER 5

SOCIAL DEVELOPMENT

> The strongest and deepest bond in the world is the dependence on our fellow men.
>
> J. Robert Oppenheimer

Subjects

5.1 The process of socialisation
5.2 Erik Erikson's psychosocial development theory
5.3 The family
5.4 Family relationships
5.5 Friendships
5.6 Educational implications for teaching and learning in a culturally diverse life world
5.7 Synthesis

Keywords

social development, socialisation, psychosocial development stages, psychological learning environment, motho ke motho ka batho, multicultural education, community education, technical education, human education, inductive education, school climate, classroom climate, family, procreation, play, child development, peer group

5.1 The process of socialisation

A person is born into a home, which translates into a family, a unit of society. A home is a special, secure space where one lives in day in and day out, and it is a source of support and strength in making his life world habitable.

To get on with others is the beginning of the formation of relationships. The child, under the guidance of the adult, will attach meaning to his/her environment and creates a network of personalized relationships. The attribution of meaning to the physical and psychological environment affords the child the opportunity to know and understand his life world.

Human relationships are characterized by amongst others, the following:

- Human beings are dependent on one another.
- Human beings want to be accepted by others.
- Human beings have a freedom of association.

Keeley (1982: 235) defines a person thus: 'I, on my own, am an individual. I, with others, am a person'. Botho means personhood is displayed only in relation to the community. Motho ke motho ka batho implies 'I am a person through other people within my community'.

As a reminder, socialisation is an adult-initiated process by which children—through education, training, and imitation—acquire the habits and values of their culture.

Husband and wife are created to live together under the guidance of mutual respect, sharing, and growth.

The ability to act in accordance to the expectations of society is a positive sign towards social development. Social development includes all social influences on knowing throughout life. Active participation or involvement assist an individual to attribute real meaning in the whole process. A positive step one has to take, is a socially acceptable behavior, namely, to learn to behave in a way the society approves. Socially acceptable behavior goes hand in love with a socially approved 'roles', namely, that members of the group have clearly defined roles which each one is expected to play.

Society has a set of approved standards which is expected that members must comply with. A positive social attitude has to be adopted for one to enjoy social activity. If one is successful in mastering this, chances are that they will integrate well with society and be accepted as such.

Language and communication coins what we refer to as a socialized speech. This only begins once a child can view a situation from another person's perspective.

Successful socialization takes the following process:

(1) The child is placed in a situation where he or she can socialize.
(2) The child becomes involved with his or her playmate (or whoever the other party may be) and the play situation.
(3) The child attributes meaning to it; for instance, by thinking, "I can play this game", or "My friend likes me", or "He is a nice friend to talk to". (This is the cognitive aspect.)
(4) The feeling arising from this is the experience (affective aspect) and it could be either pleasurable or disagreeable. This will determine the polarity effect.
(5) The polarity effect is the attraction or repulsion we feel for a person, situation or object. If the child becomes involved, attributes a positive meaning to the social situation, and this gives rise to a sense of pleasure (positive experience), then the polarity effect between the child and that social situation will be one of attraction.
(6) Next time the child may seek out the social situation spontaneously. At all events he or she will become

involved in it with greater psychic vitality, and thus the socializing gets off to a positive start.
(7) One beneficial effect of such a positive start is that children begin to evaluate themselves positively in social situations, which helps them to develop a positive social self-concept.
(8) Ultimately, we might say that in that particular social situation, the child has actualized himself or herself. (Prinsloo 1994:36).

Learning, growing, development in society is facilitated by having adequate role models. Adults will have to teach children how to behave socially and lead them in such a way that they themselves are role models and children are free to emulate them.

This activity and behavior of emulation also translate into identification or modelling. To model is to imitate certain aspects of behavior of others. Typically, modelling is explained on the basis of the reinforcing effects of imitative behavior. Identification involves an attempt to take on the values, interests, habits and characteristics of other persons (Lefrancois 1981: 115). In other words, the child uses other persons as models. These models are important for the formation of an own identity.

Myburgh & Anders (1989: 124) point out that the models in the adolescent's life are those persons with whom the adolescent should identify. The group of identification figures includes the peer group, parents, teachers and other adults mostly from the everyday life of the adolescent. A prerequisite for identification to take place is that the identification figure commands respect from the child. At first identification takes place with the person himself. This is gradually replaced by an identification with the values represented by the person.

According to Vrey (1979: 44-48) self- concept formation, identity formation and identification play a very important role in the sense that they determine the way which the child becomes and learns.

5.2 Erik Erikson's psychosocial development theory

The ability to act in accordance to the expectations of society is a positive sign towards social development. Psychosocial development relates to social development in that it includes all social and psychological influences on learning throughout life.

Rapaport(1959: 11) calls Erikson's psychosocial development theory "a theory of reality relationships". This theory is largely based on Sigmund Freud's thesis but mainly focuses on 'the process of socialization' (Maied 1968: 17).

Erikson, in his expansion of Freud's thesis, came up with a number of differences.

The following table will in brief show the differences in the two theories.

Sigmund Freud	Erik Erikson
He puts emphasis on the **id** (drives.)	He accentuates on the self (ego), attribution of meaning, and the formation of relationships.
He concentrates on the child's relations with his parents (a triangular relationship).	He views the child in a broad social context.
He concentrates on the origins of deviant behavior.	He concentrates on a successful resolution of the development crises.

(Compare Prinsloo et al. 1994: 45.)

Erikson's theory greatly focuses on the individual's instinctive drives for his inclusion in society as well as cultural influences on the ego (Zigler and Finn-Stevenson 1987: 19). This theory pivots around the fact that human development consists of the progressive resolution of conflicts between needs and social demands. Erikson theorises that an individual progresses through a series of stages. During each of these stages, the individual is confronted by crises and must deal with specific crises before progress can be made to the next set of problems. Each crisis is brought on by the specific manner in which the individual and society interact (Louw 1991: 58).

Langeveld (Mathunyane 1992: 91) mentions that four principles guide the psychosocial development of the child. These principles are:

- biological moment
- principle of helplessness
- principle of security
- principle of exploitation, which includes the principle of emancipation.

If, in the process of development, one principle impedes psychosocial development, then the development of the child will be disturbed.

Erikson's psychosocial development stages (confer Louw 1991: 58; Perkins 1969: 204; Zigler and Finn-Stevenson 1987: 204; Bergh et al. 1999: begin and progress as follows:

- Stage 1: Trust versus mistrust, the infancy stage (zero to one year). The infant is engaged here, with the trust or mistrust of the self and the environment.
- Stage 2: Autonomy versus shame, early childhood stage (one to three years). The child seeks autonomy in controlling the environment or has to subordinate his/her autonomy to the will of others.
- Stage 3: Initiative versus guilt, the play age (three to five years). Activity, curiosity, and imagination in play may be inconsistent with adult expectations, thereby creating guilt in the child. If a child is given freedom to explore and experiment, tendencies towards initiatives will be encouraged. The child can find out who he

is and what he is capable of doing if he has a certain amount of freedom to do so without feeling guilty about it (Erikson 1974: 115). It is during this period that the child intrudes himself into other people's lives and thoughts.

- Stage 4: Industry versus inferiority (five to twelve years). The child in this stage is eager to make things and to make things work. Erikson (1968: 86) feels that the child should be encouraged to be productive and encouraged to complete activities he has initiated. Kroger (1989: 25) describes industry as 'an apprenticeship to life'. It is from this apprenticeship that a feeling of competence and achievement is celebrated. Children who learn that they are skilful tend to take the sense of competence with them through adolescence; those who learn failure early tend to carry the sense of inferiority through adolescence.
- Stage 5: Identity versus role confusion (twelve to eighteen years). In this fifth stage, the child is expected to know himself, to know who he is and his way forward. This phase has been preceded by four earlier stages, each having a necessary place in the task of building an identity. During each phase, an aspect of a person's identity is formed (Erikson 1974: 180). The success of each phase contributes to a healthy achievement of identity during this fifth stage (Bester 1990: 95; Kroger 1989: 19; Stern and Eichorn 1989: 277).

According to Erikson (1968: 89), in order to find identity, the adolescent has three major factors to contend with—namely, physical growth (including appearance, sexual maturation, and accompanying urges) and the adolescent's desired perspective on his function as an adult member of society (Thornburg 1973: 3).

For successful identity resolution, the adolescent has to be faithful and committed. Commitment means adoption of an ideology (attitudes, values, and beliefs) that coincides with the behavioural prescription for one's adopted role or occupation (Lerner and Spanier 1980: 347). According to Lloyd (1985: 270), commitment is the most significant aspect of child development because it provides the child with a framework by which to integrate the various aspects of identity: self-concept, sexual role and sexuality, occupational aspirations, and related lifestyle choices.

The adolescent aims for the achievement of a hierarchy of roles or selves. His behaviour is interpreted in terms of a search for identity or a series of identities (Wall 1977: 29).

- Stage 6: Intimacy versus isolation (early adulthood). Young adults share their identity with others by affiliation and friendship. Commitment and ethical awareness are bonding aspects for successful relationships. Mutual trust, sharing spheres of work and recreation, and mutual simultaneous sexual satisfaction are characteristics of these young people.
- Stage 7: Generativity versus stagnation (adulthood). Sociality in the individual is re-energised and instils the feeling that he needs the company of others. Societal involvement and religious work are prioritised more than before, and in this way, his offspring are closer to his heart.
- Stage 8: Ego integrity versus despair (ageing/maturity). Now, the aged individual is satisfied and feels that life has been meaningful, and this good sense or feeling softens the fear of death.

5.3 The family

5.3.1 The role of the family

A family should fulfil its function as the primary life world of the child; the nuclear family should meet the general requirements.

5.3.1.1 General functions

- The father, as the head of the family, should be the undisputed authority and should be able to rely on the full support of the mother.
- Parents should mutually take responsibility for bringing up the child.
- The child has a deep need for authority and discipline and should experience these within the family.
- The child should be prepared by the family for life and the future by regular religious attendance.
- The family should be the primary societal unit, and getting along with the other members of the family should be a major concern (Verster et al. 1982: 42).

5.3.1.2 Supplementary functions

These functions are the embellishers of the family:

- Husband and wife sexual needs are satisfied and It is a unit for the production of off springs, and
- Both father and mother cooperate in the provision of resources and finances for the family (Goode 1982 : 13–14).

5.3.1.3 General features

The following are the general features of the nuclear family:

- It resides in the separate dwelling that is not shared by the other relatives of the married couple.
- It is economically independent of the broader system of relatives.
- It devotes its primary and first loyalty exclusively to the married couple and their dependents.
- It is autonomous, with authority in its own circle and an emphasis on the privacy of the family.
- It is, despite its autonomy, in contact with a wide-ranging network of relations maintained by mutual support (Prinsloo and Du Plesis 1998: 65).

5.3.1.4 Parental practices affecting child development

Parents generally exercise different parenting styles that are associated with child development, and the different kinds of parents are:

➢ Authoritative parents enforce clear rules and reward compliance.

> Authoritarian parents exert control without passion.
> Indulgent parents are warm and caring parents with little guidance and discipline.
> Neglectful parents totally abdicate parental responsibilities (Passer et al. 2001: 429).

5.3.2 Procreation: Sexuality in the family

God gave man a precious gift—sexuality. This gift was supposed to be enjoyed and used properly because it serves as the foundation of an enduring, rich, and loving relationship. This gift is not revocable due to its bonding function. This special relationship ties the family and has the following functions:

- offers the experience of a loving, intimate, and consistently dependable relationship fused with personal warmth (I–you relationship)
- ensures the physical and material provision, care, health, and safety of its members
- recognises its task with respect to the socialisation of children and the promotion of their personal development and capabilities
- offers support to children in the acquisition of independence and their establishment of a marriage and family life of their own (Prinsloo and Du Plesis 1998: 55).

This partnership may or may not be blessed with children. Now this family of three or four has to function as a unit, and for this to happen, all members of the family will have to assume different roles, duties, and responsibilities (for each of them to perform) except for the fact that the father remains the head, leader, and manager of the family.

5.3.3 The father, the head of the family

A husband becomes a good father by taking his tasks seriously. These tasks are:

- The father must take responsibility of the decisions he makes irrespective of how dire the consequences are.
- The father must be prepared for the sake of his family to lose some of his personal freedom.
- The father must be prepared to take some roles performed by his wife during the pregnancy period.
- The father must accept the fact that the child will be accommodated into his family space, time, and social life.
- The father must acknowledge that the arrival of the baby means that he must expect the extended family to occupy some of his space. Now grandparents, aunts, and uncles will invade his free space, and he himself will realise that he has been someone's son and now he is someone's father.
- All in all, the father must become a place of refuge for all. His behaviour should instil a sense of trust in him, and he must quickly learn that his wife nor children are not perfect. But he has to act like a parent by accommodating these weaknesses and put appropriate corrective measures (Gerdes et al. 1981: 188).

On this last point, its man's belief that God is a parent and knows his children. God says children naturally do silly, careless things, but a good spanking (not assault) will teach them how to behave (Proverbs 22:15). And if you don't punish your son, you don't love him. If you do love him, you will correct him (Proverbs 13:24). Corrections mean to show the child his/her unacceptable or unbecoming behaviour, and discipline is good for him/her (Proverbs 29:18).

At the same time the father has to learn to be a good listener. Communication is a solution to many problems. This skill of listening demands active involvement with children whether it is playing, praying, hanging out, and going to church together. The togetherness is good and will assist in understanding your children and developing trust, obedience, and a feeling of security.

Job in the Bible portrays a father who is responsible, caring, loving, faithful, obedient, and protective, an example all fathers must follow. Every morning, Job would get up early and offer sacrifices for each of his children in order to purify them. He always did this because he thought that one of them might have sinned by insulting God *unintentionally* (Job 1:5).

5.3.4 Parents' (father and mother) relationship

This relationship is strictly based on love, and the Lord directs that husbands must love their wives and be polite with them, that wives have to submit to their husbands (Colossians 3:18–19), and that their love for each other must extend to their children by bringing them up as a family with strict but warm discipline.

Children or a newly born child will change the lifestyles of their parents. The parents' relationship changes from a two-way affair to that of a triangle. In some cases, this new development has disturbed their communication and intimacy; their leisure time is reduced as it has become a child-centred affair, adding new responsibilities, like taking turns to look after their children, and adding an extra financial burden (Gerdes et al. 1981).

Oops! There's also a reduction of sexual intercourse. Ah! Maybe a Moses crib can be a solution!

The Lord advises parents to carry each other's burden, and in this way, they will be obeying the law of God (Galatians 6:2).

The two parents must *form* a united front for the education of their children. Van Schalkwyk (1979: 35) endorses the view that basic education takes place in the family, and therefore, a family must take care of the child. It is the task of the family to support and aid the children in his growth towards maturity, and the relationships a child has with his community are to a great extent influenced by the relations he has with his family. The parents, by sending the child to school, take the responsibility of cooperating with the school in the education of the child (Mathunyane 1992: 78).

5.3.5 The role of the extended family.

"The extended family is composed of the members of a series of immediate families inhabiting the same locale." It includes a man and his parents, brothers, bother's wives, sons, unmarried daughters and other relatives.

In the evenings the adolescents enjoy listening to their grandparents relating traditional legend. Grandparents are regarded as adequately qualified teachers to lay the foundations for education that will prepare the adolescent to live happily and comfortable and to be useful to his society (McFadden & Gbekobou 1984: 225). Usually, grandparents are the best informed, the most patient and most readily accessible resource for young ones who are able to react naturally in their presence. In such truly friendly relationships, learning takes place easily (Lekhela 1958:19).

The education received from grandparents ensures a good sense of identity and also gives the adolescent a chance to develop acceptance and adoption of the norms and values of the community.

5.4 Family relationships

Big family, grandparents and children.

5.4.1 Children and the home

The family is regarded as the pre-eminent socialisation context because the child's earliest experiences occur within this situation and much time is consumed in family interactions (Hartup and Moore 1990: 1). Relationships within families offer a wide variety of interactions and are vehicles of understanding social and cultural issues.

The parent-and-child relationship is assumed to be important for the transmission of cultural standards, values, and rules to the child (Dekovic 1992: 1). As part of their integration into society, children have to acquire certain norms and values of their culture through the process of socialisation.

Children feel sufficiently confident if their relationship with their parents is sound. Thus, confidence allows them to move out from the parents' secure base to engage in new situations and relationships (Denham et al. 1991: 39). According to Burns (1986: 161), children's adjustments to life depend on their subjective interpretation of their family's treatment of them and on conditions within the family. Therefore, it is evident that the psychological atmosphere of the home plays a very important role in the formation of a basis for other institutions in which children will be involved in later life.

Social influence emanates from the home environment and manifests itself, amongst others, in the following ways:

- Family relationships affect social adjustments outside the home.
- Role-playing in the home sets the pattern for role-playing outside the home.
- Home training is responsible for gender role typing. What gender role stereotypes children learn and how well they learn to perform them outside the home is greatly influenced by the home training they have received.
- Family relationships develop children's personalities. What older children think of themselves is a direct reflection of what they believe different family members think of them and is judged by the way they are treated by members of the family (Hurlock 1993: 184).
- Parents influence children's emotional growth. The emotional link between children and parents is strong and appears to have a considerable influence on children's social adjustment.
- Children learn socially acceptable behaviour from parents. Cooperation, obedience, responsibility, and neatness are examples of behaviours which are observed and adopted by children. The verbal and non-verbal behaviour of parents is inculcated in children and results in well-adjusted children.

> The traditions and habits of the family are transmitted to children by parents. These are learned by children through imitation. Good and acceptable habits assist children to adjust well outside the home (Mathunyane 1996: 84).

5.4.1.1 Older siblings in the family

Relationships between brothers and sisters are vitally important because they can have a lasting influence on development and on the individual's ultimate adult personality and roles (Rice 1984: 394). The importance of the siblings' relationships are highlighted below (Mathunyane 1992: 36–37):

- Older siblings are likely to serve as role models for younger brothers and sisters. They may effectively teach young siblings about identity problems, sexual behaviour, and physical appearance. They set examples for character, personality traits, and overall behaviour by the type of person they are. This has a strong influence on the development of younger brothers and sisters.
- Older siblings often serve as surrogate parents, acting as caretakers, teachers, playmates, and confidants. Pleasant relationships can contribute to younger children's sense of security, belonging, and acceptance. Hostile, rejecting relationships may create deep-seated feelings of anxiety, insecurity, resentment, or hostility. If older children feel they are displeased by younger siblings and are refused the attention and care formerly given to them, they may carry this feeling of displacement, jealousy, and competition into adulthood. If, however, older children feel useful, accepted, and admired because of the care they give younger children, this added appreciation and sense of usefulness contributes positively to their own sense

of self-worth. Many adolescents learn adult roles and responsibilities by having to care for younger brothers and sisters while growing up.
- Siblings often provide companionship and friendship and meet one another's needs for affection and meaningful relationships. They act as confidants for one another, are able to help one another when there are problems, and share many experiences. Siblings, out of necessity, have to learn to share, to consider one another's feelings and desires, and to deal with differences.

5.4.1.2 Grandparents

Grandparents-and-children relationships serve as a bridge between the separated generations. This relationship can have very positive effects on children.

- Grandparents contribute to the children's emerging sense of identity by providing continuity in linking the past to the present family roots and thus having a positive impact on the adolescent's search for identity (Fuhrmann 1986: 69).
- Grandparents may have a positive impact on parent–child relations by conveying information about parents to the children. Children also turn to grandparents as confidants and arbiters when they are in conflict with their parents (Rogers 1985: 235).
- Grandparents help children understand ageing and acceptance of the aged. Children who see their grandparents frequently and have a good relationship with them are more likely to have positive attitudes towards the elderly (Rice 1984: 396).

5.4.1.3 The influence of tradition and culture in the family

The traditional family includes the children, parents, grandparents, uncles, brothers, sisters, and other immediate relatives who may have their own children (Mbiti: 1971: 106). Education is transmitted to the child by senior members of the family. Emphasis is on the acceptance of norms and values of the father, who have similarly inherited them from his father.

The father is expected to give his son the education necessary to make him productive and a proper carrier of the family name. The mother, on the other hand, sees to it that her daughter maintains the cultural standards set for all decent girls who, as a result, experience little difficulty in finding an understanding husband and establishing a home. African fables, proverbs, and legends, orally told by parents and other older adults, are clear examples of a society's effort to transmit value to the youth (Mathunyane 1992: 65).

5.5 Friendships

5.5.1 Sociality

Rogers (1985: 264) defines friendship as an 'ongoing reciprocal and behavioural involvement between two individuals'. Children often select friends on the basis of proximity and similarities. The presence of different genders and cultural, ethnic, and socio-economic groups may affect grouping patterns.

The study of boys and girls in play (Erwin 1993: 162) reveals differences between the play of boys and girls. It was found that boys play outdoors more often than girls. The social play of boys is based on larger groups than that of girls. The social group of boys are more diverse in age than those of girls. Girls are more likely to play predominantly male games than boys are to play girls' games. Boys play competitive games more often than girls do and tend to control the larger spaces designated for such activities. Boys' games last longer than girls' games. The proportion of child–child interactions spent in play varies from culture to culture.

Adolescents' peer groups are usually organised into cliques, which are small groups of between two and twelve individuals (the average is about five or six) generally of the same sex and age.

Cliques play a vital role in structuring adolescents' social activities. Occasionally, several cliques—some boys and girls or boys and girls as single-sex groups—come together for social activities, forming a larger, more loosely organised crowd. Crowds are usually composed of about three or four cliques or approximately twenty individuals (Lloyd 1985: 199).

Adolescents who belong to no cliques or crowds or who gain little satisfaction from organised groups may join a gang. Gang members are usually of the same sex, and their main interests is compensating for peer rejection through antisocial behaviour (Hurlock 1980: 232).

Steinberg (1985: 166) maintains that among the informal adolescent groups, cliques provide the adolescents with a sense of identity by serving as a basis of comparison or as a referring group. Through comparison, clique members learn about themselves and evaluate their experiences in school, at home, and in the broader peer group.

Another way in which cliques serve as reference groups is in providing the members with an identity in the eyes of other adolescents. Adolescents judge one another on the basis of the company they keep. They become branded on the basis of whom they hang around with. Clique identities are important because they become the basis for an adolescent's own identity.

Take, for example, two boys whose clique is held together by a common dislike of school. By having their attitude towards school continually reinforced by one another, the boys' feelings about school become strengthened, and not liking school becomes a part of each boy's identity. Even if something very positive happens at school, it becomes difficult for someone in the clique to admit that it makes him feel good about himself (Steinberg 1985: 167).

Religious parents should advise children about friends and quote Ecclesiastes 12:1, 'Remember your creator while you are still young; and keep company with the wise … do not make friends with people who have hot, violent tempers. You might learn their habits and not be able to change' (Proverbs 22:24–25).

5.5.2 Play, the best teacher

In any group, members are expected to conform to the ideas and values consistent to the culture of childhood, which consist of children's play. Play provides children with opportunities of acquiring information and skills that lay a foundation for learning. Play enables children to advance to new developmental stages and to deal with life experiences, which they attempt to respect, master, or negate. Play also involves self-teaching and self- healing, for in the play situation, children can make up for frustrations and defeats in the real world.

Through play, children learn what no one can teach them; therefore, play functions as a resource for education (Wakefield 1979: 14). Play, amongst others, empowers a child in the following ways:

- Play is symbolic and meaningful. This means that play represents reality. The symbols and values attributed to play are a reflection of the child's culture.
- Play is active and pleasurable. This means that children engage in an activity with others and enjoy themselves. Children at play exchange feelings and interact freely to an extent that a sense of belonging is developed.
- Play is episodic. Children's roles and goals change and develop based upon their experiences in society. When teachers share captivating stories with children and invite them to act out such stories, the dramatisation is carried over into play. Teachers can make abstract ideas, such as social equity, concrete for children through dramatisation of non-fiction and fiction books (Vold 1992: 54–56; Mathunyane 1996: 86–87).

5.5.3 The influence of a peer group in child development

Children by all means struggle for their emancipation and attempt to conform to their peers in every respect. The peer group directs child development in one or more ways:

- The peer group fulfils the need for friendship, especially for children who do not find much affection at home.
- The peer groups offer children the security they previously experienced from their parents. They, therefore, facilitate emancipation by balancing the need for independence and dependence.
- The peer group gives children the opportunity to practise social skills and to experiment with new ideas, behaviour, and attitudes.
- The peer group facilitates the transfer of knowledge and information as well as help the child to adapt and obey social rules and regulations.
- The peer group helps to reinforce gender roles.
- The peer group is a group of equals. Competition within a group takes place on an equal footing.
- Acceptance in the peer group enables the child to form a positive self-concept, which in turn develops into self-dignity.
- Friends can help young people acquire a clear, stable identity in a number of ways, namely:
  - They assist adolescents in resolving their conflicts within themselves and with others.
  - They teach them respect for competence, which is necessary for the acquisition of maturity and autonomy.
  - They teach them how to act in social situations, especially those involving heterosexual relationships.
- The peer group offers its members the opportunity for intimate relationships.
- Recreational activities always form part of this group. Such activities are usually informal, often relatively inexpensive, and generally unsupervised by adults. These activities are important to the adolescent's social development because they offer opportunities

for young people to develop leadership and autonomy, to test them socially, and to establish their own values (Louw 1991: 364–365; Vrey 1979: 104; Mathunyane 1992: 41; and Lambert et al. 1978: 70–71).

5.5.4 The development of heterosexual relationships

Rice (1984: 309) defines heterosexuality as 'the stage of development in which the individual's pleasure and friendship are found with those of both sexes'. The adolescent's interest in sex grows. The adolescent is passionately eager to form intimate relationships with members of the opposite sex. Getting acquainted and feeling at ease with the opposite sex is a painful process for some adolescents because during the earlier puberty stage, boys and girls develop attitudes of resentment against members of the opposite sex.

Sexual maturity comes with a biological awareness of the opposite sex as well as an interest in activities in which they are involved. The new interest is romantic in nature and is accompanied by a strong desire to win the approval of members of the opposite sex. The boy's first effort is to tease by engaging in some sort of physical contact with the girl—for example, pulling her hair, hitting her with a snowball. Her response is often culturally conditioned and predictable—for example, screaming, running, and pretending to be very upset. The boy is not very good at talking to girls, but he knows how to roughhouse, so he uses this time-honoured method of making his first emotionally charged heterosexual contact (Rice 1984: 309; Hurlock 1980: 245).

This is the period where children and parents clash most of the time as children move towards greater independence and self-determination.

Parents will keep on advising the child or youth about his/her friends. The parent will always say to boys, 'Be careful of girls.' On the other hand, they say to girls 'Be careful of boys.'

5.5.5 The influence of tradition and culture in the peer group

Respect for older persons is a traditional value carried over from one generation to another. Krige (Schapera 1967: 96) points out that, at an early age, children learn not to sit or eat with people older than themselves. They spend most of their time with those of their own age, playing together or working together, and are recognised by their elders as a group, from which collective responsibility for herding and other occupations is expected. As a child grows, he comes into contact with an ever-widening circle of people, which first includes other children in the neighbourhood and, later, at the circumcision school or in the regiment. The significance of these encounters is great in that selfishness, bad temper, and other faults are constantly checked by the group. The younger children are also strictly controlled by the group just older than themselves.

Initially, the boys are responsible for herding, for bird-scaring, and so on. Admission into the initiation school and/or to the regiment becomes important because his knowledge widens and responsibilities become greater. The content taught is important for him as an individual and for the community in which he lives.

In the same way, girls have to start at an early age to help their mothers grind corn and fetch water and kindle wood. These feminine activities are also performed communally, and older girls control the activities of those younger than themselves. A great deal of inculturation rests in these youth activities (Monnig 1967: 107).

5.6 Educational implications for teaching and learning in a culturally diverse life world

There are two educational structures, namely, the family as the educationally interested structure, and the school as educationally qualified structure.

(a) The family as the educationally interested structure.

Van Schalkwyk (1979: 35) says that the family must be a true community of love for the adolescent. It must take care of the adolescent. It is the task of the family to support and aid the child in his growth towards maturity. Basic education takes place in the family. But since the family is not structured for the complete opening up of the child, it depends on the school. The relationships an adolescent has with his community are to a greater extent influenced by the relations he has with his family. The parent, by sending the child to school, takes the responsibility of cooperating with the school in the education of the child. There should be regular contact between the home and the school. In other words, the parent must be responsible and support the school and on the other hand, the school must be willing for the parent to watch over the quality and spirit of its activities. The rights of the child should be acknowledged...

(b) The school as educationally qualified structure.

A child to be brought into the mainstream of school life, has to be involved in the work and activities of the school.

His learning activities must challenge rather than frustrate him. He must be helped to achieve status within the group. Through a classroom activities and sports, he should be given the opportunity to identify closely with the school. The support he gets from his teachers and peers will cause him to think of himself in a certain way as a student. Motivation which will lead him to improved academic achievement will be generated.

In a school environment, the teacher is a professional role model for the learners. His personal example will influence value systems, dress, time-keeping and behavior.

The following points may demonstrate the influence of the teacher on learning.

- His personal qualities and competence.
- Successful teachers are always energetic, self-confident, concerned, humanitarian and innovative.
- Warm, friendly and emotionally involved teachers are best-liked.
- In order to influence learners positively, the teacher has to strive for their mental health.
- To maintain sound relationships, teachers must praise those who do well and encourage those who struggles.
- The teachers has to know the child. He has to know his home, background, and has to keep accurate records of his progress.
- The teacher must interact with the parents and community

Apart from the teacher's role, the peer group also plays a major role in the education of the child.

Peer group acceptance in the school situation is very important since it is related to academic success. If the child is poorly accepted by the peer group, he is likely to underachieve. His obsession about his peer groups will be at the expense of his school work. This is so because the peer group's values and norms exert an important influence on this life, development and behavior.

5.6.1 The principles of teaching and learning in a culturally diverse school environment

Education in a multicultural and multireligious society amounts to a carefully programmed induction into the complexity of society and lays the foundations of learning to cope with the complexities of tomorrow. The few principles that underlie the above notion are outlined below (Mathunyane 1996:26 – 29).

5.6.1.1 The principle of differentiation

The principle of differentiation is the principle of recognising differences and variety in life, which includes differential education of the child and differentiated unfolding of reality. This indicates that if a child in a plural society is not exposed to that kind of differentiation, then he or she cannot properly accept his cultural mandate (Claassen 1989: 34).

5.6.1.2 The principle of integration

The principle of integration recognises that unity in diversity must be accounted for in the total educational system. In learning, the child must acquire not only a basic knowledge of his culture but also knowledge of other lifestyles (Claassen 1989(b) 35; Abbey et al. 1990: 9).

According to Coutts (1992(b) 97), integration implies that adaptations are made by one cultural group in order to 'fit in' with the dominant cultural group without completely disregarding their own culture (Hessari and Hill 1990: 10).

Watson (1988: 542) maintains that integration ensures equal opportunity accompanied by cultural diversity in an atmosphere of mutual tolerance and the maintenance of positive intergroup relations (Bagley and Verma 1983: 8).

5.6.1.3 The principle of continuity

The principle of continuity is derived from the recognition of the importance of the past for an understanding of the present. It emphasises the continuing significance tradition has for a sense of cultural identity. On the other hand, it allows for reflection, for adaptation, and for changes to meet present needs. It allows, in other words, for decision-making and facilitates personal choices.

The principle is directed towards developing the critical and evaluative faculty in children, stage by stage, so that the decisions they make and the opinions they come to hold are informed and reasonable (Hulmes 1989: 153).

5.6.1.4 The principle of assimilation

The principle of assimilation is where ethnic minorities are absorbed over the course of time into the mainstream of the dominant group in society. The affected ethnic group is expected to adopt the language, cultural modes (dress), and values of the host society.

Schooling can be used to good effect to ensure assimilation because there is official insistence on the use of one language to teach one set of social values and customs (Hessari and Hill 1990: 9; Watson 1988: 537).

5.6.2 Objectives of education in a cultural diverse society

Claassen (1989(a) 432) indicates that education in a culturally diverse society should be education which accounts for cultural diversity in a positive manner and that it is a universal kind of education for all students. Claassen further points out that this education is desirable in that the school population reflects the plural composition of society.

5.6.2.1 General objectives of education in a culturally diverse society

Banks (1991–1992: 32) says the objectives of education within the pluralistic society should affirm and help children understand their homes and the community culture.

Education must help students to:

- free students from their cultural boundaries
- acquire the knowledge, attitudes, and skills they will need to participate in civic action in order to make society more equitable and just.

\Various researchers point out the following as the general objectives of multicultural education in a democratic society:

- This education enables children to develop towards maturity with the ability to recognise inequality, injustice, racism, stereotypes, prejudice, and bias. This equips them with the knowledge and skills to help them challenge and attempt to change these manifestations when they encounter them in all strata of society (Hessari and Hill 1990: 30) and to open their minds to the fact of diversity within themselves, within others, and within the national society (Hessari and Hilll 1990: 4),
- This aims at alerting the pupils to the varied world around them and also to inculcate cultural respect,

THE DICHOTOMY: FACTS AND PERCEPTIONS

which is the educational spearhead of a drive against racism and intolerance (Baruth and Lee Manning 1992: 24; Beckmann 1992: 6; Edwards 1991: 939).
- This must make members of a cultural group aware of their own culture (Claassen 1989(b) 55).
- This must combat discrimination (Claassen 1989(b) 60).
- This aims at the creation of an educational environment in which a wide range of cultural groups (such as gender, ethnic, and various regional groups) will experience educational equality (Baruth and Lee Manning 1992: 24; Goodey 1988: 15–16; McCormick 1984: 94).
- This should provide an environment that recognises differences among people, perceives cultural differences as strengths rather than weaknesses to be remediated, and emphasises the importance of all differences and exceptionalities in the education process (Baruth and Lee Manning 1992: 23).
- This must ensure that students do not have any inherent bias towards other cultures and that they are encouraged to find interest in different world views and examine these views critically, absorbing what they find to be of worth and value (Oliver 1990: 26).
- This aims at preparing pupils to live harmoniously in a multicultural society and to strive to bring about or maintain a just society for all. Pupils must realise that cultural diversity benefits the society and that cross-cultural interaction is a normal, healthy human endeavour. Pupils must learn that being different does not mean being inferior and that every citizen has a right to participate and contribute to every sphere of life regardless of sex, social status, religious affiliation, or skin colour (Brown 1982: 12).
- This must enable students to understand as many subcultural groups as possible (Claassen 1989(b) 61).

To summarise the above-mentioned aims, it can be said that, in general, multicultural education aims at providing a richer educational environment in terms of cross-cultural knowledge and understanding, removing artificial barriers, and creating wider perspectives in our society (Mathunyane 1996: 26–29).

5.6.2.2 Specific objectives of education in a multicultural society

There are three specific objectives of education in a multicultural society. Hulmes (1989: 20–22) states these objectives, as distinguished by Paul Tillich, as being:

- √ **Technical education**
  Tillich (Hulmes 1989: 20) associates technical education with the acquisition of knowledge and skills (some of them quite basic, others much more sophisticated) in the use of tools. Every society requires the service of well-trained technicians and skilled craftsmen for multiplicity of services. One aim of education is to produce such skilled individuals in sufficient numbers.

- √ **Humanistic education**
  Education in a multicultural society aims at aiding the child to actualise his potentialities, both generally and individually. The aim of the educational process is the development of the humanistic personality in which as many potentialities as possible are matured, among them being technical skills and religious function.

- √ **Inductive education**
  The induction of children into their families—with their traditions, symbols, and demands—is the basic form of induction education.

Its aim is not the development of the potentialities of the individual but his or her induction into the actuality of a group, the life and spirit of the community, family, tribe, town, nation, and church. Such a process happens spontaneously through the individual's participation in the life of the group. The truth of it seems to be that these three aims of education—namely, the technical, humanistic, and inductive—are closely interdependent. In the final analysis, all education is inductive in the sense that it helps to introduce individuals into what for them are new aspects of the mystery of human existence (Mathunyane 1996: 29).

5.6.3 Creation of a psychologically safe learning environment

Creating the most favourable climate for learning is a challenge to teachers because of various factors being involved, such as interpersonal relationships, attitudes of children, and the development of the teachers' own ability to interact with people from different cultures. A multicultural classroom climate is a fully established environment that reflects and respects racial, cultural, gender, ability, and age diversity through classroom design, use of curriculum, and social personal interactions. Sound interactions will create a psychologically safe environment (Claassen 1992 160) For a healthy, informative, and educative learning environment to exist, the teachers, children, and parents have important roles to play (Mathunyane 1996:35-39).

5.6.3.1 Teachers: Excellence in action

In order to provide quality instruction, teachers have to provide a warm and safe environment, and children have to receive expressions of esteem and positive regard from the teachers. Good teachers express caring for the children, advocate for them in relationship negotiation with other children, and generally respond to them as they would with their own child.

A good teacher has authority. Authority, within the context of multicultural schooling, is intimately linked to the manner in which teachers exercise control, direct, influence, and make decisions about what is actually to take place in their classrooms (Darder 1991: 107).

Children attend school to learn to solve problems, to make mistakes, and to learn from them in a positive environment.

Some children exhibit consistent cooperative behaviour, while others are a daily challenge to the patience of teachers.

The multicultural classroom transmits the message each day to each child that the opportunity exists to change and to improve under the direction of an understanding teacher.

At the same time the teacher—through his control, direction, and influence—has to create opportunities for children to develop a sense of industry and self-efficacy. Good teachers know how to orchestrate the activities of children so that they experience successes in a variety of tasks. They also know how to recognise special efforts and to encourage special abilities.

Good teachers will always share with parents and children common cultural assumptions and experiential backgrounds (Perry et al. 1993: 241).

According to Vold (1992: 68–70), teachers in the execution of their duties will have to ensure that the climate of their classroom is observably multicultural. In order to maintain such a classroom climate, Fennimore (Vold 1992) suggests the use of the AVIMA (accept, value, identify, model, and advocate) model, which provides a conceptual guideline enabling teachers to analyse and focus their attitudes and subsequent classroom and social behaviour.

The model outlines the following steps:

- Teachers *accept* the diversity in their classroom (compare Drake 1993: 264).
  Teachers *value* the diversities as a challenge to successful preparation of all children for life in a multicultural world and are determined to find the valuable skills and attributes of all children (compare Claassen 1992: 160). The ability to decide for oneself about accepting or rejecting a particular set of beliefs or attitudes in life is an acquired skill. This has a bearing on the role of teachers in a pluralistic society. That is, they will have to work towards reaching a point where their pupils

are able to think for themselves, weigh the evidence, and then make a decision on the basis of that evidence.
- Teachers identify and articulate exactly what they can accomplish for their students regardless of diversities (such as learning disabilities, unemployed parents) and those which might be perceived as discouraging negatives.
- Teachers willingly *model* excellence, acting as school leaders in terms of their positive and productive approach to diversity.
- Teachers *advocate* for children through design of classroom interaction, peer interaction, and social interaction that might impact on the acceptance and positive valuing of their children (Mathunyane 1996: 37).

Grossman (1991: 161–162) concurs with Perry et al. (1993) and Vold (1992) by emphasising that for teachers to achieve the intended objectives of multicultural classrooms, they will have to acquire cultural sensitivity, meaning that they should be aware of the effects of these differences, and cultural literacy. They will have to acquire a detailed knowledge of the cultural characteristics of a specific ethnic and socio-economic group and, in some cases, also be aware of the attitudinal and behavioural changes.

Teachers who do not agree that they need to be culturally literate when working with a group of ethnically and socio-economically diverse children will have to change their attitudes about how to deal with diversity among children.

5.6.3.2 Community education

A school belongs to the parents and the immediate community. It is important that efforts be made to get parents involved in the education of their children. Parents and other community members should be aware of what is happening at school, and they should feel that their contributions and opinions are sought and respected.

As parents become involved in education and learn more about the society's goals, there is likely to be more overall support and assistance in the general affairs of the school (Baruth and Lee Manning 1992: 190). Parents function as helpers, experts, decision makers as well as teachers in the home. Parents are co-planners of the educational welfare of their children and are also responsible for the provision of an environment and atmosphere conducive to learning and development.

One other important function of a parent in the promotion of a warm classroom climate is to become a real 'home teacher'. Parents who read stories to their children and expose them to multiple pictures of different people, cultural materials, and so on expose children to (and prepare them for) the expectations of the social environment (Orr 1992: 21).

5.6.4 The collaboration of the 'trio' (home, general community, and s chool) towards successful learning

Parenting styles are highly associated with the child's educational development. Children with authoritative parents tend to have higher self- esteem and do well in school.

Children with authoritarian parents seldom perform well as they have a low self-esteem. Indulgent and neglectful parents are not taking care of their children properly and thus their children become a liability to society.

Mathunyane (1996: 75–78) highlights the fact that the quality of children's educational life in school is determined by how well the socialisation in school matches, fortifies, and builds on their experiences at home. Parents should relate stories and hang pictures and posters that highlight variations in lifestyle, work, religion, age, and appearance and should refer to these as normal features of life; children will easily absorb information about others and be able to adjust and control their life environment.

According to Martin (1990: 62), for an educational situation to arise, it is necessary for the teacher and the child to interact and have a social contact. If this relationship is sound, then it indicates that the child's image is respected. The role the teachers have to play in this relationship is to facilitate learning, to help the child acquire social skills, to stimulate self- actualisation, and to expand the child's environment (compare Prinsloo et al. 1996: 120–122).

The school creates opportunities for the children to participate in activities that will encourage their awareness of others. For instance, a variety of work can be done to help children to get to know others at school, both children and adults, with whom they will come into either regular or infrequent contact, such as those they meet outside the classrooms, administrative staff, and members of the community.

The contact children make in the school and community extend their 'selves' to include the objects, people, institutions, ideas, beliefs, and values with which they identify.

THE DICHOTOMY: FACTS AND PERCEPTIONS

Clemes and Beans (Abbey et al. 1990: 15–19) address the cultural relevance of self-esteem in children by pointing out that positive self-esteem can be attained when children experience positive feelings in the following fields:

- Connectivity: This relates to the feeling children have when they derive satisfaction from the company of others. Satisfaction can be derived from identifying with a group of people, feeling connected to a past heritage, feeling that they belong to something or someone, feeling good about their relation or affiliation, and knowing that the people or groups they are related to are considered in a positive light by others and feel important to others.
- Uniqueness: This is the special sense of self children feel when they can acknowledge and respect qualities or attributes that make them special and different when they receive respect and approval from others for these qualities. Children feel unique by being aware that others think they are special. They are able to express themselves in individual ways, they respect themselves as individuals, and they enjoy the feeling of being different without having to make others uncomfortable.
- Models: These are reference points that provide children with human, philosophical, and operational examples that help them establish meaningful values, goals, ideals, and personal standards.

Parents and community leaders provide models of strength and accomplishment in situations relevant to children and display models worth emulating.

The way teachers cope with their emotions within a social context influence children to develop:

- pride within their families, friends, community, and school
- a sense of connection among children by developing a climate of mutual respect
- a view of their culture as a source of value and pride
- a positive self-identity and the appreciation of their culture as a positive aspect of who they are.

It is educationally sound that the school should give children the opportunity to choose their friends independently and must also create ample opportunity for social contact on the part of the child. The school must utilise children's prosperity for social interactions in their daily programmes—for instance, holding group competitions, such as class quizzes and debates—and must enforce safety and security through strict but warm discipline. Children feel safer when they know what behaviours are expected and feel sure that they will be protected from others' misbehaviour.

The interactions children experience with parents, teachers, and the community (people of various cultural groups) have a positive impact on their learning, becoming, self-esteem, and social development.

5.7 Synthesis

The home is the source of cultural standards, habits, values, and rules to the child.

A warm and nurturing home environment becomes a vehicle for understanding social issues, and therefore, children feel secure and sociable in their relations with other adults and children. Adults who are concerned about the development of their community should participate in school activities and provide children with recognisable role models.

Children's interactions with their friends and their engagement in a number of social activities contribute towards their independence from the family life.

Their experiences in the school environment give children the opportunity to understand other peoples' lives and facilitate a supportive role towards school learning and socialisation in general.

A nation is, first of all, rich in its people.

Rich in man.

Rich in youth.

Rich in every individual. Pope John Paul II

REFERENCES

Abbey, N., Brindis, C., and Casas, M. 1990. *Family Life Education in Multicultural Classrooms*. Santa Cruz and California: ETR Associates.

Alexander, P., and Alexander, D. 1973. *The Lion Handbook to the Bible*. England and Australia: Lion Publishing and Albatross Books.

Bagley, C., and Verma, G. K. 1983. *Multicultural childhood*. England: Gower.

Baker, G. C. 1979. 'Policy Issues in Multicultural Education in the United States'. *The Journal of Negro Education*, XLVIII: 253–266.

Banks, J. A. 1991–1992. 'Multicultural Education: For Freedom's Sake'. *Educational Leadership*, 49/4: 32–36.

Baptiste, H. P., and Baptiste, M. L. 1979. *Developing the Multicultural Process in Classroom Instruction: Competences for Teachers*. University Press of America.

Baruth, L. G., and Lee Manning, M. 1992. *Multicultural Education of Children and Adolescents*. USA: Allyn and Bacon.

Beckmann, J. L. 1992. 'Multikulturele Onderwys: 'n Terreinverkenning'. *Journal for Technical and Vocational Education*, 135: 5–10.

Behr, A. L. 1975. *Psychology and the School*. Pretoria: Van Schaik.

Bent, R. K. 1970. *Principles of Secondary Education*. New York: McGraw-Hill Book Company.

Beresford, D. 1999. 'The Flawed Visionary of New Africa (A Profile of Thabo Mbeki)'. *The Guardian*, 9 January 1999. <http://en.wikipedia.org/wiki/I_Am_an_African?oldid=659570840> accessed 13 June 2015.

Bergh, Z., Theron, A., Albertyn, L., Badenhorst, F., Geldenhuys, D., Ungerer, L. Cilliers, F., and Dekoker, T. 1999. *Psychology in the Work Context*. UK: Oxford University Press.

Bester, G. 1990. 'Die gebruik van Erikson se personlikheidsteorie vir die meting van identiteitsvorming by skoolgaande adolessente'. *Educare*, 19/1, 2 : 90– 96.

Board, J. C. 1991. *A Special Relationship: Our Teachers and How We Learned*. New York: Pushcart Press.

Brown, E. J. 1982. 'Multicultural Education: A Challenge Today'. *Transvaal Education News*, 80/9: 10–13.

Budhal, R. S. 2000. 'The Impact of the Principal's Instructional Leadership on the Culture of Teaching and Learning in the School'. MEd dissertation. Pretoria: University of South Africa.

Burnhill, L., Rubenstein, G., and Rocklin, N. 1979. 'From Generation to Generation: Fathers-to-be in Transition'. *The Family Coordinator*. 28(2)229–235.

Burns, R. B. 1986. *Child Development: A Text for Caring Professions*. New York: Nichols.

Case, R. 1973. 'Piaget's Theory of Child Development and Its Implications'. *Phi Delta Kappa* 55/1: 20–25.

Cilliers, J. L. Le R. 1975. *Education and the Child*. Durban: Butterworth. Claassen, J. C. 1989a. 'Multikulturele onderwys: feite en mite'. *South African Journal of Education* 9/3: 429–433.

—— 1989b. 'Multikulturele onderwys: 'n Studie in die vergelykende opvoedkunde'. DEd-proefskrif. Bloemfontein: Universiteit van Oranje- vrystaat.

Claassen, J.C. 1992. Riglyne vir die implementering van multikulturele onderwys in die R.S.A. South African Journal of Education 12(2): 106- 111.

Clasen, D.R. 1992. Stategies for enhancing learning in the multicultural classroom. International Journal of Special Education 7(2):159-163.

Coan, R. W. 1987. *Human Consciousness and Its Evolution: A Multidimensional View.* Westport, Connecticut: Greenwood.

Cohen, L., and Manion, L. 1983. *Multicultural Classroom: Perspective for Teachers.* London and Canberra: Groom Helm.

Cole, L., and Hall, I. N. 1970. *Psychology of Adolescence.* New York and Chicago: Holt, Rinehart and Winston Inc.

Collins, W. A. 1984. *Development during Middle Childhood: The Years from Six to Twelve.* Washington DC: National Academy Press.

Conger, J. J. 1991. *Adolescence and Youth: Psychological Development in a Changing World.* Harper Collins Publishers Inc.

Constitution of the Republic of South Africa 1996. Pietermaritzburg: Interpark Books.

Coutts, A. 1992a. 'Multicultural Education'. *Mentor*, 74/1: 8–11.

—— 1992b. *Multicultural Education: The Way Ahead.* Pietermaritzburg: Shuter and Shooter.

Coutts, A. 1990. The multicultural school. Mentor 72(4):5-10.

Craig, G. J. 1983. *Human Development.* Englewood, NJ: Prentice-Hall.

Daloz, L. A. 1986. *Effective Teaching and Mentoring.* San Francisco: Jossey Bass.

Darder, A. 1991. Culture and power in the classroom. New York: Bergin & Garvey.

Dekovic, M. 1992. *The Role of Parents in the Development of Child's Peer Acceptance.* Assen-Maastricht: Van Gorcum.

Denham, S. A., Zahn-Waxler, C., Cummings, E. M., and Iannotti, R. J. 1991. 'Social Competence in Young Children's Peer Relations: Patterns of Development and Change'. *Child Psychology Human Development*, 21/1: 29–44.

Dictionary of South African English 1996. New York: Oxford University Press.

Dipboye, R. L., Smith, C. S., and Howell, W. C. 1994. *Understanding Industrial and Organisational Psychology: An Integrated Approach*. Fort Worth: Harcourt Brace College Publishers.

Disasa, J. 1988. 'African Children's Attitude towards Learning'. *Journal of Multicultural Counselling and Development*, 16/1: 16–24.

Dollar, C. 2011. *Winning in Troubled Times*. New York: Faith Words.

Du Toit, S. J., and Kruger, N. 1991. *The Child: An Education Perceptive*. Durban: Butterworths.

Edwards, J. 1991. 'Literacy and Education on Contexts of Cultural and Linguistic Heterogeneity'. *Canadian Modern language Review*, 47: 933–949.

Elkins, D. N., Hedstorm, L. J., Hughes, L. L., Leaf, J. A., and Saunders, C. 1988. Towards a Humanistic Phenomenological Spirituality'. *Journal of Humanistic Psychology*, 28/4: 5–18.

Engelbrecht, P., Krigler, S. M., and Booysen, M. I. 1996. *Perspectives on Learning Difficulties: International Concerns and South African Realities*. Pretoria: J. L. Van Schalk Publishers.

Erikson, E. H. 1963. *Change and Challenge*. New York: Basic Books Inc. Publishers.

––– 1968. *Identity and Life Cycle*. New York: International Universities Press.

––– 1974. *Identity Youth and Crisis*. London: Faber & Faber.

Erwin, P. 1993. *Friendship and Peer Relations in Children*. Chichester and New York: John Wiley & Sons.

Felhaber, T. and Mayeng, I. 1997. *South African Traditional Healer's Primary Health Care Handbook*. Cape Town: Kagiso.

Fowler, F. G., and Fowler, H. W. 1969. *The Pocket Oxford Dictionary of Current English*. Oxford: Clarendon Press.

Fuhrmann, B. S. 1986. *Adolescence, Adolescents*. Boston and Toronto: Little, Brown and Company.

Fullan, M. 1997. *Leadership and the Moral Purpose of Schools in South Africa Vol. 1: Selected Themes in Education Management Development*. Toronto: McGill University. (Canada–South Africa Education Management Program).

Garrison, D. R., and Archer, W. 2000. *A Transactional Perspective on Teaching and Learning: A Framework for Adult and Higher Education*. Oxford: Elsevier Science.

Gerber, P. D., Nel, P. S., and Van Dyk, P. S. 1998. *Human Resource Management*. Johannesburg: Thompson.

Gerdes, L. C., Ochse, R., Stander, C., and Van Ede, D. 1981. *The Developing Adult*. Durban and Pretoria: Butterworth and Co. (SA) (Pty) Limited.

Ginsburg, I. H. 1982. 'Jean Piaget and Rudolf Steiner: Stages of Child Development and Implications for Pedagogy'. *Teachers College Record*, 84/2: 327–337.

Good News Translation (GNT). 1992. 2nd edn, American Bible Society. Goode, W. J. 1982. *The Family*. Englewood Cliffs, New Jersey: Prentice-Hall.

Goodey, J. S. 1988. *Multicultural Education in South Africa: Is It Possible?* Pretoria: University of South Africa.

Gorman, R. M. 1974. *The Psychology of Classroom Learning: An Inductive Approach*. Columbus and Ohio: Merrill Publishing Company.

Gunter, C. F. G. 1977. Aspects of educational theory. Stellenbosch: University Publishers & Booksellers.

Hammond, M., and Collins, R. 1991. *Self-Directed Learning: Critical Practice*. London: Kogan Page.

Hartup, W. W., and Moore, S. G. 1990. 'Early Peer Relations: Development Significance and Prognostic Implications'. *Early Childhood Research Quarterly*, 5/1: 1–17.

Herskovits, M. J. 1966. *Man and His Works: The Science of Cultural Anthropology*. New York: Alfred A. Knopf.

Hessari, R., and Hill, D. 1990. *Practical Ideas for Multicultural Learning and Teaching in the Primary Classroom*. London: Routledge.

Hulmes, E. 1989. *Education and Cultural Diversity*. London and New York: Longman.

Hurlock, E. B. 1973. *Adolescent Development*. New York: McGraw-Hill Kogakusha Limited.

―― 1980. *Developmental Psychology: A Lifespan Approach*. New York: McGraw-Hill Book Company.

Hutchinson Concise Encyclopaedic Dictionary. 1992. London: Helicon. Ivancevich, J. M., and Matteson, M. T. 1993. *Organisational Behaviour and Management*. 3rd edn, Homewood: Irwin.

Johnson, D.E. 1968. Expanding and modifying guidance programmes. Boston: Houghton Mifflin company.

Kavanagh, K. 2002. *South Africa Concise Oxford Dictionary*. Oxford: University Press.

Keeley, R. 1982. *The Lion Handbook of Christian Belief*. England and Australia: Albatross Books.

Kegan, R. 2000. 'What "Form" Transforms? A Constructive Developmental Approach to Transformative Learning', in Mezirow, J. and Associates (eds), *Learning as Transformation: Critical Perspectives on a Theory in Progress*. San Francisco: Jossey-Bass, 35– 70.

Kendall, F. E. 1983. *Diversity in the Classroom: A Multicultural Approach to the Education of Young Children*. New York and London: Teachers College Press-Columbia University.

Krige, E. J. and Krige, J. D. 1965. *The Realm of a Rain Queen: A Study of the Pattern of Lobedu Society*. London: Oxford University Press.

Kroger, J. 1989. *Identity in Adolescence: The Balance between Self and Other*. London and New York: Routledge.

Kuper, H. 1986. *The Swazi: A South African Kingdom*. New York: Holt, Reinhart and Winston Inc.

Lambert, B. G., Rotchild, B. F., Altland, R., and Green, L. B. 1978. *Adolescence: Transition from Childhood to Maturity*. Belmont and California: Wadsworth Publishing Co. Inc.

—— 1989. 'Accepting Others' Values in the Classroom: An Important Difference'. *Clearing House*, 62/4: 273–274.

Landsberg, E. 2005. *Addressing Barriers to Learning: A South African Perspective*. Pretoria: Van Schaik Publishers.

Lekhela, E. P. 1958. 'The Development of Bantu Education in the North- Western Cape (1840–1847): An Historical Survey'. MEd dissertation. Pretoria: University of South Africa.

Le Roux, J. 1993. *The Black Child in Crisis: A Socio-Educational Perspective*. Pretoria: J. L. Van Schaik.

—— and Pretorius, J. W. M. 1992. *Themes in Socio-Pedagogics*. Pretoria: J. L. Van Schaik.

Lerner, R. M., and Spanier, G. B. 1980. *Adolescent Development: A Life- Span Perspective*. St Louis and New York: McGraw-Hill Book Company.

Lloyd, M. A. 1985. *Adolescence*. New York: Harper and Row Publishers. Louw, D. A. 1991. *Human Development*. Haum Tertiary.

—— and Edwards, D. 1993. *Psychology: An Introduction for Students in Southern Africa*. Johannesburg: Lexicon Publishers.

Lutheran Study Bible (LSB) 2009. New Revised Standard Version, Minneapolis: Augsburg Fortress.

Maier, H. W. 1968. *Three Theories of Child Development*. New York: Harper.

Magwa, M. L., Cooposamy, M. R., and Mayekiso, B. 2001. 'A Comparison of the Relationship between Modern/Western and South African Indigenous Approaches to Medicinal Plant Utilisation'. Department of Botany & Electron Microscope Unit. University of Fort Hare.

Makgopa, M. 2001. 'Indigenous Healing System: An Oral Transmission. Department of Northern Sotho'. University of Venda for Science and Technology.

Mandela, N. Online 2015. 'I Have Cherished the Ideal'. <https://www.nelsonmandela.org/news/entry/i-am-prepared-to-die> accessed 14 June 2015.

Martin, C. J. 1990. *The Changing Image of the Child in South Africa*. MEd dissertation. Pretoria: University of South Africa.

Masoga, M. and Musyoki, A. 2001. 'Building on the Indigenous: An African Perspective: Proceedings of an International Conference on Indigenous Knowledge Systems'. Thohoyandou and Pretoria: University of Venda for Science and Technology and National Research Foundation (International Conference: 12–15 September 2001).

Mathunyane, L. H. 1992. 'Pupil Identity Formation with Special Reference to the Black Adolescent'. MEd dissertation. Pretoria: University of South Africa.

—— 1996. 'Relationship Formation in Multicultural Primary School Classrooms'. DEd thesis. Pretoria: University of South Africa.

—— 2015. *Christian Identity Formation: The Contemporary Lutheranism*. UK: Lightning Source UK Ltd/Partridge Publishing Company.

Mbiti, J. S. 1971. *African Religion and Philosophy*. London: Heinemann. McCormick, T. E. 1984. 'Multiculturalism: Some Principles and Issues'. *Theory into Practice*, 23: 93–97.

McFadden, J., and Gbekobou, K. N. 1984. 'Counselling African Children in the United States'. *Elementary School Guidance and Counselling*, 18/3: 225–230.

Mclean, B., and Young, J. 1988, *Multicultural Anti-racist Education: A Manual for Primary Schools*. UK: Longman Group.

Meynell, A. 'The Shepherdess'. <http://www.poemhunter.com/poem/the- shepherdess/> accessed 14 June 2015. And <http://poetry.elcore.net/CatholicPoets/Meynell/Meynell036.html> created 08 April 2001, accessed 14 June 2015.

Miller, D. R., Belkin, G. S., and Gray, J. L. 1982. *Educational Psychology: An Introduction*. Dubuque and Iowa: Wm. C. Brown.

Moloi, K. C. 2002. *The School as a Learning Organisation: Reconceptualising School Practice in South Africa*. Pretoria: Van Schaik Publishers.

Monnig, H. O. 1967. *The Pedi*. Pretoria: Van Schaik.

Montefiore, S. S. 2010. *Speeches that Changed the World*. London: Quercur Publishing Plc.

Mufamadi, J. 2001. 'Diagnosing and Treatment of Mental Illness in South Africa: Cultural Considerations'. University of Venda for Science and Technology.

Napoli, V., Kilbride, J. M., and Tebb, D. E. 1988. *Adjustment and Growth in a Changing World*. St. Paul: West.

Nicholls, A. and Nicholls, S.H. 1983. Developing a curriculum- A practical guide. London: George Allen & Unwin (publishers) Limited.

Obama, B. CNN Online. 'That Timeless Creed'. <http://edition.cnn.com/2008/POLITICS/11/04/obama.transcript/> accessed 14 June 2015.

Oberholzer M. O., Landman, W. A., Higgs, P., Roelofse, J. J., Swanepoel, E. M., and Barnard, F. 1993. 'Only Study Guide for OFO411-K'. Pretoria: University of South Africa.

Oliver, P. 1990. 'Multicultural Education: A Concept Analysis'. *Vocational Aspects of Education*, 42/111: 25–28.

Orr, J. 1992. Facilitating language development in a multicultural playroom. Kleuterklanke 17(2):21-24.

'Papalia, D. E., and Olds, S. W. 1993. *A Child's World: Infancy through Adolescence*. New York: McGraw-Hill.

Parrinder, G. 1954. *African Traditional Religion*. Cape Town: Hutchinson's University Library.

Passer, M. W., and Smith, R. E. 2001. *Psychology: The Science of Mind and Behaviour*. New York: McGraw-Hill Companies Inc.

Perkins, H. V. 1969. *Human Development and Learning*. Belmont and California: Wadsworth.

Perry, T. and Fraser, J.W. 1993. Freedoms plow: Teaching in the multicultural classroom. New York: Routledge.

Pitje, G. M. 1950. 'Traditional Systems of the Male Education among the Pedi and Cognate Tribes'. Part I and II. *African Studies*, 9, 2, and 3.

Pius, X. I. 1936. *The Christian Education of Youth*. New York: The American Press.

Plunkett, W. R. 1975. *Supervision: The Direction of People at Work*. Dubuque, IA: Brown.

Popenoe, D. 1986. *Sociology*. Englewood Cliffs: Prentice-Hall.

Prinsloo, E., and Du Plesis, S. 1998. 'Socio-Education I'. Pretoria: University of South Africa.

—— Vorster, P. J., Sibaya, P. T., and Mathunyane, L. H. 1996. 'Teaching with Confidence: Psychology of Education for Southern Africa'. Pretoria: Kagiso Tertiary.

—— Wiechers, E., Kokot, S. J., Olivier, A., and Van Ransburg, J. J. J. 1994. 'Only Study Guide for OSI431-5'. Pretoria: University of South Africa.

Pullias, E. V., and Young, J. D. 1968. *A Teacher Is Many Things*. Bloomington: Indiana University Press.

Ramabulana, A. V. 2001. 'The Role of Initiation Schools in Dealing with Unplanned Teenage Pregnancy in Thohoyandou'. University of Venda for Science and Technology.

Ramsey, P. G. 1991. *Making Friends in School: Promoting Peer Relationships in Early Childhood*. New York and London: Teachers College Press.

Rapaport, D. 1959. 'A Historical Survey of Psychoanalytic, Ego Psychology', in Erikson, E. H. (ed.) *Identity and the Life Cycle*. New York: International University Press

Raum, O. F. 1967. 'An Evaluation of Indigenous Education', in Duminy, P. A. *Trends and Challenges in the Education of the South African Bantu*. Van Schaik.

Redden, J. D., and Ryan, F. A. 1956. *A Catholic Philosophy of Education*. USA: The Bruce Publishing Company.

Rice, F. P. 1984. *The Adolescent Development, Relationships and Culture*. Boston and London: Allyn and Bacon Inc.

Rogers, D. 1985. *Adolescents and Youth*. New Jersey: Prentice-Hall Inc. Sadler, W. S. 1948. *Adolescence Problems: A Handbook for Physicians, Parents, and Teachers*. St. Louis: The C. V. Mosby Company.

Santrock, J. W. 1984. *Adolescence: An Introduction*. Dubuque: Wcb.Wm.C. Brown Publishers.

Schapera, I. 1967. *Western Civilization and Native of South Africa*. London: Routledge and K. Paul.

Sheldon, K. 2005. Historical dictionary of women in sub-Saharan Africa. Toronto:The Scarecrow Press, Inc.

Smith, E. W. 1950. *African Ideas of God*. London: Edinburgh House Press. Sohnge, W. F. 1992. *Educare*, 21/1, 2. Pretoria: University of South Africa.

Shryock, H. 1983. *Your Medical Guide*. All-Africa Publishers. Stark, R. 1975. *Social Problems*. Washington: Random House. Steinberg, L. 1985. *Adolescence*. New York: Alfred A. Knopf.

Stern, D., and Eichorn, D. 1989. *Adolescence and Work: Social Structure, Labour Markets, and Culture*. New Jersey: Lawrence Erlbaum Associates Publishers.

Stone, H. J. S. 1981. *The Nature and Structure of the School*. Pretoria and Cape Town: Academia.

Stone, R. 1984. *The Good Teacher: How Teachers Judge Teachers*. New York: Philosophical Library.

Sybouts, W., and Krepel, W. J. 1984. *Student Activities in the Secondary Schools*. Westpost: Greenwood Press.

Tappert, T. G., Pelikan, J., Fischer, R. H., and Piepkorn, A. C. 1959. *The Book of Concord: The Confession of the Evangelical Lutheran Church*. Philadelphia: Fortress Press. The Holy Bible, English Standard Version (ESV). 2001. Crossway Bible, a Division of Good News Publishers.

Thompson, F. 1908. *Selected Poems of Francis Thompson*. London: Methuen and Co. Ltd.

Thornburg, H. 1973. *Adolescent Development: Introduction to General Psychology: A Self-Selection Textbook*. Dubuque: W. M. C. Brown Company Publishers.

Van der Horst, H. R. 1993. 'Differentiated Introduction and the Multicultural Classroom'. *Educare*, 22/1, 2: 32–37.

Van Den Aardweg, E. M., and Van Den Aardweg, E. D. 1988. *Dictionary of Empirical Education/Educational Psychology*. Pretoria: E. and E. Enterprises Arcadia.

Van Deventer, I., and Kruger, A. G. 2003. *An Educator's Guide to School Management Skills*. Pretoria: Van Sckaik Publishers.

Van Schalkwyk, O. J. 1979. *Educare: Journal of Faculty of Education (Unisa)*, 8.1, 8.2: 30–36. Pretoria: University of South Africa. Verster, T. L., Theron, A. M. C., and Van Zyl, A. E. 1982. *Educational Themes in Time Perspective: Part 1*. Durban: Butterworths.

Vold, E. B. 1992. *Multicultural Education in Early Childhood Classrooms*. Washington: National Education Association.

Vrey, J. D. 1979. *The Self-Actualising Educand*. Pretoria: University of South Africa.

Wakefield, P. 1979. 'Happiness Is a Bilingual-Bicultural Child'. *Prime Areas*, 21/3: 12–14.

Wall, W. D. 1977. *Constructive Education for Adolescents*. London: Unesco Harrays.

Watson, J. K. P. 1988. 'From Assimilation to Anti-Racism: Changing Educational Policies in England and Wales'. *Journal of Multilingual- Multicultural Development*, 9/6: 531–552.

World Health Organisation (WHO). 1993. 'Life Skills Education for Children and Adolescents in Schools'. Geneva.

Yamamoto, K. 1988. 'To See Life Grow: The Meaning of Mentorship'. *Theory to Practice*, XXVII/3: 183–189.

Zigler, E. F., and Finn-Stevenson, M. 1987. *Children: Development and Social Issues*. Toronto: D. C. Heath.

Ingram Content Group UK Ltd.
Milton Keynes UK
UKHW011937230423
420518UK00008B/56